# BEYOND THE PEN

## Mastering Artificial Intelligence
## to create successful books

DANIEL GROSLEAU

# Table of Contents

# Foreword

Writing a novel has long been considered an almost mystical process, reserved for an elite of authors gifted with undeniable natural talent. However, the dazzling advances of artificial intelligence are shaking up this traditional conception of creative writing. Now, each of us has the opportunity to embark on the captivating adventure of creative writing, thanks to these valuable narrative assistance tools.

While some purists still balk at the idea, I'm convinced that there's no need to have the slightest embarrassment or complex about using AI to help you write your novel. After all, the greatest writers have always been able to surround themselves with external resources to feed their imagination and perfect their art.

This new approach is in no way a form of cheating or reductive ease. On the contrary, it opens up unsuspected creative perspectives and allows more talented people to make their literary dreams come true. Your pen will remain the backbone of your story, while AI will play a role as an informed advisor.

Because let's not be so naïve as to think that artificial intelligences alone will be able to generate an authentic novelistic masterpiece. A bestseller worthy of the name must be carried by a true author's vision, a solid artistic direction and a coherent narrative breath over time. This is precisely where your role as a human creator will remain crucial and decisive.

Thanks to AI, the tedious task of finding every word, every sentence, every guiding idea will be greatly lightened. This genius assistant will propose hundreds of creative avenues in the blink of an eye that you can then explore, modulate or reject according to your feelings. It's then up to you to determine the course to follow, to infuse that personal touch essential to the resonance of a great work.

Rather than getting lost in the twists and turns of the blank page, you'll devote your time and energy to shaping the subtle architecture of your novel. Developing endearing characters with complex psychologies, imagining twists and turns capable of keeping your readers on the edge of their seats, building immersive universes of unparalleled richness - these will be your new priorities as AI-augmented writers.

Far from short-circuiting the creative process, you'll instead make a tenfold creative effort to transcend the raw proposals of your virtual assistant. This stimulating challenge will require total and uncompromising artistic involvement from you. The path to writing excellence will always require long hours of reflection, deletion, and reworking to refine your vision.

Becoming a best-selling author is certainly not an easy path. But the fascinating opportunities offered by artificial intelligence will make this exhilarating quest for creative self-realization within the reach of countless new talents. It's up to you to seize this incredible opportunity and embark on one of the greatest adventures of all: breathing life into a novel destined to make an impression.

# Chapter 1

# Introduction to Writing by Artificial Intelligence

## What is Artificial Intelligence (AI)?

Artificial intelligence (AI) has revolutionized many aspects of our daily lives, and the field of writing is not to be outdone. AI has transformed the way authors approach their work and has opened up new avenues to boost creativity and optimize productivity.

Among the main contributions of AI to writing are the tools and software specifically designed to assist authors in their creative process. These tools use sophisticated algorithms to analyze and understand textual data, offering suggestions for words, phrases, and even ideas to improve the quality of written content. Spell and grammar checkers are a common example of these tools. They rely on AI-based language models to detect grammar and spelling errors, allowing authors to perfect their work and avoid clumsiness.

Another area where AI plays a critical role is content generation. AI-based text generation models are capable of producing coherent, natural-looking sentences that resemble those written by humans. These templates are often used to create automated content, such as article summaries or even entire articles. However, it is important to emphasize that these models are complementary tools and cannot replace the talent and creativity of authors. They are there to inspire and support, but not to substitute for individual artistic expression.

AI can also be leveraged to help authors better understand their target audience. Through data analysis and machine learning, AI algorithms are able to identify trends and preferences among readers, providing valuable insights to guide the writing process. This allows authors to tailor their content according to their audience's expectations, improving their reception and impact.

Artificial intelligence offers many opportunities to improve the quality of writing and boost creativity. AI-based tools are there to assist authors, enable them to better understand their audience, and optimize their productivity. However, it is crucial not to lose sight of the importance of individual artistic expression and to view these tools as allies, rather than replacements, for human creativity.

# The Emergence of AI-Powered Writing Tools

The last few years have marked a transformation in the art of writing with the advent of writing tools powered by artificial intelligence. They are revolutionizing the way writers work by providing support and innovative perspectives. By automating routine aspects and suggesting original ideas, these advancements improve both the quality and efficiency of writing.

AI solutions for writers, such as advanced text generation systems and natural language processing tools, stand out for their ability to understand and manipulate language with remarkable finesse. These technologies offer a range of services, from tone analysis to translation, helping authors refine their prose and expand their creativity.

The rapid rise of these platforms opens up a world of possibilities, allowing writers to tap into the potential of AI to enrich their creative process and explore new literary avenues.

## Optimize the writing process

Writing is an art that requires time, concentration and a certain rigour. Every writer knows how difficult it can be to find inspiration, structure their ideas, and perfect their text. However, thanks to artificial intelligence (AI), it is now possible to optimize and streamline the writing process.

An essential aspect of AI in the writing process is content generation. AI-based text generation models are capable of producing paragraphs, articles, and even complete stories. These models use sophisticated algorithms to analyze and understand textual data, allowing them to generate consistent and compelling content. This feature can be extremely valuable for authors who need to quickly produce content for specific projects, such as product descriptions, article summaries, or even scripts for videos.

In addition to facilitating correction and content generation, AI can also be used to simplify the process of searching for information. AI-based search engines are able to sort and rank search results based on their relevance and reliability. This allows authors to quickly find the most relevant information for their work, avoiding wasting time browsing through many websites. In addition, AI can also help in the collection and organization of data from different sources. This allows authors to benefit from simplified access to a wealth of information, allowing them to enrich their content and deepen their knowledge on a given topic.

Another benefit of AI in the writing process is its role in assisting with planning and structuring. AI-based *mind mapping* tools  allow authors to visualize and organize their ideas visually. By linking concepts and sub-themes, these tools make it easier to create a clear and logical structure for the text to come. Additionally, AI can also suggest headings, subheadings, and sections, providing a solid framework for organizing content. This allows authors to save time by avoiding blockages and hesitations related to the planning and structuring of their text.

**AI allows authors to become more efficient and produce higher quality work.**

Artificial intelligence (AI) is a powerful tool that offers authors new perspectives to improve their efficiency and the quality of their work. This is because AI-powered tools, such as spell and grammar checkers, text generation models, and data analysis algorithms, are designed to help writers optimize their creative process and better understand their target audience.

With these tools, authors can benefit from suggested words, phrases, and ideas to enrich their content and make it more engaging for readers. AI-based spell and grammar checkers use advanced language models to detect grammar and spelling errors, allowing writers to polish their text and avoid awkwardness that could hinder the understanding and appreciation of their work.

Additionally, AI-based text generation models are capable of producing coherent and natural sentences that resemble those written by humans. These templates are often used to create automated content, such as article summaries or even entire articles. While these role models cannot replace the talent and creativity of authors, they are there to inspire and support them in their work.

Finally, data analytics and machine learning allow AI algorithms to better understand reader trends and preferences, providing valuable insights to guide the writing process. This way, authors can tailor their content according to their audience's expectations, improving their reception and impact.

In short, artificial intelligence offers many opportunities to improve the quality of writing and stimulate creativity. AI-based tools are there to assist authors and help them better understand their audience. It is important for writers to continue to explore their own ideas and express their worldview through their works, using AI-based tools as allies to optimize their creative process.

**Correction & Suggestion Tools**

One of the main uses of artificial intelligence (AI) in the writing process is autocorrect and text suggestions. AI-based spell and grammar checkers have become essential companions for authors, helping them avoid grammar and spelling mistakes.

When we write, it's common to make grammar or spelling mistakes. This could be due to haste, unfamiliarity with language rules, or simply a distraction. Whatever the reason, these mistakes can damage the quality and credibility of our work. That's where AI comes in. AI-based spell and grammar checkers are designed to detect these errors and offer accurate corrections.

Using sophisticated algorithms, these tools are able to analyze text and spot common mistakes such as spelling, punctuation, conjugation, or syntax mistakes. They are also able to detect more subtle mistakes, such as misusing a word or constructing an awkward sentence. AI takes into account the context in which the text is used, allowing it to offer suggestions that match the author's style and intent.

The major advantage of these AI-based spell and grammar checkers is their ability to provide instant corrections. When we write on a computer or mobile device, these tools are often integrated with word processing software, web browsers, or messaging apps. This means that we can receive correction suggestions in real-time, without having to interrupt our workflow. This not only saves time, but also reduces the effort required to revise and improve our text.

Moreover, these tools are not limited to simply correcting errors. They also offer text suggestions to improve the style and clarity of the content. For example, they can offer alternatives for repeated words or phrases, suggest rephrasing to make a sentence more concise, or offer advice on the structure of a paragraph. These suggestions are based on linguistic models and grammar rules, but also on the analysis of large amounts of already published texts.

It's important to point out that these AI-based spell and grammar checkers aren't foolproof. Although they are extremely accurate, they can sometimes fail to detect certain errors or offer corrections that are not appropriate for a specific context. Therefore, it is always necessary to use your best judgment and carefully proofread your text, even after using these tools.

Another major benefit of artificial intelligence (AI)-based tools is their ability to adapt to each author's individual writing style. This is because these spell and grammar checkers, as well as text generation templates, learn from their users' writing habits and adjust accordingly. Over time, they become more and more accurate in their suggestions and in detecting specific mistakes that each writer tends to make.

This allows for continuous improvement in the quality of writing and a reduction in recurring errors. It's essential to keep in mind that AI is constantly evolving and learning continuously. The more information we provide to her, the more she adapts to our writing. At the beginning of using these tools, it is important to guide them and let them know our preferences for tone, sentence structures, and other stylistic elements.

This way, the AI will be able to capture the essence of each author's writing style and tailor the text according to their unique flavor. This adaptation allows writers to receive personalized support and optimize their creative process, while maintaining their own voice and writing style. All in all, AI-based tools offer valuable and adaptive help for authors, allowing them to focus on creating compelling and well-structured stories.

## Content Generation

Automated content generation offers multiple benefits. First of all, it saves time. Rather than having to manually write each paragraph or article, one can use these tools to quickly produce coherent, quality content. This can be especially useful in situations where one needs to generate a large amount of content in a short period of time, such as writing product descriptions for an e-commerce site or creating content for social media.

In addition, these AI-based tools are able to adapt to different tones and writing styles. For example, they can generate formal content for news articles, but also adopt a more casual and informal tone for social media posts. This versatility makes it possible to obtain content tailored to different contexts and audiences.

One of the concerns with automated content generation is the quality and accuracy of the information produced. While these tools are capable of producing well-written text, it's important to verify the information they provide. AI can be influenced by the data it has been trained on, and this can lead to errors or biases. Therefore, it is always necessary to verify and validate the information generated by these tools.

Despite these limitations and concerns, there's no denying that automated content generation offers significant benefits. It saves time and produces consistent, high-quality content, which can be very useful in many areas. However, it is essential to find the right balance between the use of these tools and human intervention.

**Automated content**

Automated content generation is a major advancement in the field of AI, especially in the writing of blog posts. Using sophisticated algorithms, text generation models are able to understand and analyze huge amounts of textual data. They can then use this knowledge to generate text consistently and fluently.

One of the most obvious advantages of automated content generation is its speed. Instead of spending long hours manually writing paragraphs or articles, one can simply provide instructions to the AI and get generated content in a matter of moments. This is especially useful in situations where time is of the essence, such as when creating content for a last-minute marketing campaign or to meet an urgent demand for content on social media.

In addition, AI-based text generation templates are extremely versatile. They can adapt to different writing styles and produce content in a variety of tones. Whether you need formal, academic text or more casual, conversational content, AI can meet your needs.

**Automated search**

AI can also be used to make it easier to find information. AI-based search engines are able to sort and rank search results based on their relevance and reliability. This allows authors to save time by directly accessing the information that is most relevant to their work. Additionally, AI can also help with the collection and organization of data from different sources, allowing authors to have a complete set of information for their writing.

Traditional search engines have evolved significantly thanks to the integration of AI. AI-based search algorithms are able to analyze and understand the content of web pages in a more sophisticated way. They take into account many factors such as relevance, source authority, freshness of information, and even the context of the research.

This means that authors can get more targeted search results that are relevant to their specific needs. For example, an author searching for information on a specific scientific topic can get results from reliable and recent academic sources, rather than having to sort through a multitude of less relevant results.

Moreover, AI can also help solve the problem of information overload. With the explosion of data available online, it has become increasingly difficult for authors to find relevant and reliable information. AI-based search engines are able to sort and filter results based on relevance and reliability, allowing authors to focus on the information that is most useful for their work.

Artificial intelligence (AI) provides authors with valuable tools to help them create compelling and well-researched historical narratives. This is because AI can play a vital role in researching and verifying information for novels that are set in the past or a specific period of history. Thanks to its sophisticated algorithms, AI is able to analyze and understand textual data, offering writers suggestions for words, phrases, and even ideas to enrich their content and make it more realistic and believable.

In this way, AI can help authors better position their characters in the chosen historical context and accurately describe the places, events, and customs of the relevant period.

At the beginning of creation, writers can instruct the AI to take into account a specific time in the story, so that all historical references, descriptions of characters and locations are consistent and in line with the chosen time period.

For example, for a novel set during World War I, the author might say to the AI, "For this novel, the story takes place during World War I. All historical references, descriptions of people and places should take into account this period of time." The AI would then be able to provide suggestions for vocabulary, phrases, and ideas that fit the chosen era, allowing writers to create more immersive and authentic stories for their readers.

In short, artificial intelligence offers authors new perspectives to explore history and create captivating and well-researched narratives. AI-based tools allow writers to focus on storytelling and creating memorable characters, while also leveraging AI knowledge and skills to enrich their work and make it more believable and realistic.

An added benefit of using AI to facilitate information retrieval is its ability to collect and organize data from multiple sources. AI-based tools have the ability to analyze and extract information from text, images, videos, and unstructured data. This allows authors to access a comprehensive range of information from a variety of backgrounds, which greatly enriches their writing and establishes their credibility. Note that you can guide the AI in a way that favors certain trustworthy sources rather than relying on random sources. For example, you might ask, "For this novel about the human genome, consider only reliable scientific sources. Act like an expert in human genomes. You can also refer to the website of the *National Human Genome Research Institute*[1] and other similar websites.

---

[1] https://www.genome.gov/human-genome-project

By leveraging AI's data processing and analysis capabilities, you can leverage a variety of sources such as academic articles, expert reports, podcasts, documentaries, and blogs. This will not only allow you to multiply the wealth of information infused into your story, but also to guarantee a better authenticity and greater relevance of your content. What's more, using a diverse range of media will help to energize and vary the pace of your storytelling, further captivating your readers' attention and promoting an optimal reading experience.

However, it is important to note that the use of AI to make it easier to find information is not without limitations. AI-powered search engines are only as good as the data they've been trained on. If they have not been exposed to diverse, high-quality sources, they may provide biased or incomplete results. It is therefore essential to exercise good judgment and verify sources to ensure the reliability of the information.

AI-based search engines allow authors to quickly and efficiently access the information that is most relevant to their work. Additionally, AI can help in the collection and organization of data from different sources, providing a complete set of information for writing. AI is a valuable tool, but it must be used wisely and as a complement to human intelligence.

**Use a precise style**

Thanks to its colossal and ever-growing database, Artificial Intelligence (AI) has a unique ability to rely on a specific literary style or author's signature. That's because AI can tap into these existing styles and merge them harmoniously with your personal touch, providing a hybrid look that's both faithful and distinctive. Imagine, for example, that you want to compose a novel in the style of Agatha Christie; it would be enough to communicate this intention to the AI at the beginning of the process: "For this novel, I want to use a writing style similar to Agatha Christie's." The AI will then work to adapt your writing style to the famous novelist's singular prose, generating a seamless and compelling manuscript.

In addition, by opting for such a strategy, you not only benefit from being immersed in the style of a proven author, but you also inject a dose of freshness and originality by combining it with your own narrative vision. The balance between these two dimensions will be decisive in the production of captivating content, capable of titillating the imagination of readers and arousing their interest.

At the same time, it is important to mention that AI can be particularly useful for reproducing classic or ancient literary styles that are difficult for contemporary authors to grasp. Indeed, thanks to its massive processing and analysis capability, AI can dissect and interpret these complex stylistic registers, allowing writers to fully immerse themselves in these fascinating universes. Whether you want to adopt the epistolary style of Alexandre Dumas, the lyrical poetry of Victor Hugo or the naturalism of Zola, AI is a valuable guide and facilitator, conducive to the exploration of these distant yet exciting literary lands.

In short, the combination of your personal writing style and the stylistic expertise offered by AI represents a fertile symbiosis that is conducive to the development of your creativity.

# Chapter 2

# The Limits of AI in Writing

## AI and the Challenges of Writing

While artificial intelligence has limitations in the field of writing, it is also crucial to recognize its inability to fully grasp the emotional aspects and tone of a text. Human emotions are complex and nuanced, often difficult to interpret even for individuals. AI, despite its advances, struggles to understand and reproduce these emotional subtleties in writing, which can lead to texts that seem flat or disconnected from real feelings. Authors use tone and emotion to establish a connection with the reader, an ability that AI cannot yet convincingly match.

One of the main limitations of AI in writing is its lack of creativity. AI is programmed to analyze and process existing data to generate suggestions or responses. However, it lacks the capacity for innovation and originality that human authors can bring to their writings. Writing is a form of artistic expression that requires unique human understanding and sensitivity. AI can be a valuable tool, but it can't replace human creativity and intuition.

Another major challenge for AI in writing is its difficulty in understanding the context and nuances of a text. Natural language processing algorithms used by AI can struggle when it comes to grasping the deeper meaning of a text or interpreting idioms, puns, or metaphors. As a result, AI can sometimes produce inappropriate results or misinterpret the author's intent. Authors must therefore remain vigilant and exercise their judgment in evaluating the AI's suggestions.

There are also concerns about the impact of AI on the editing and review process. While AI can identify grammatical or stylistic errors, it may not be able to recognize the beauty of a unique writing style or a deliberate author's choices that deviate from conventional norms. Subjectivity in the art of writing is an essential component that contributes to the richness and diversity of literature. Relying too heavily on AI for editing risks losing those unique qualities that give each work its distinct character.

In addition, AI may also encounter limitations in less common languages. AI models are often trained on large amounts of data in popular languages, which can limit their accuracy and performance in other, lesser-studied languages. When working with less common languages, it's important to consider these limitations and rely on other resources to ensure the quality of writing.

In addition, the use of AI in writing raises ethical and bias issues. The algorithms used by AI are often trained on existing datasets, which may reflect cultural or social biases. This can result in biased suggestions or results in texts produced by the AI. So, it's crucial to take these considerations into account and critically evaluate when using AI in writing.

Nevertheless, it is important to note that AI continues to evolve and improve. Researchers are actively working to overcome these limitations, developing more advanced models that can better understand and reproduce the complexity of human writing. By incorporating more sophisticated approaches, such as deep learning and enhanced natural language processing, the future of AI in writing looks bright. In the meantime, it remains essential to balance the use of AI with human expertise and creativity to produce texts that are both accurate and emotionally resonant.

Despite these limitations, it's important to emphasize that AI can be a valuable tool for authors. The suggestions and corrections provided by AI can help improve the clarity and accuracy of texts. However, it is essential not to rely solely on AI and to maintain an active role as an author to ensure the quality and authenticity of the writing.

# Lack of creativity and human intuition

One of the most significant limitations of AI in writing is its lack of creativity and human intuition. While AI can come up with ideas and suggestions, it can't replicate the originality and emotion that human authors can bring to their writing.

Writing is a form of artistic expression that requires unique human understanding and sensitivity. Authors are able to tap into their experiences, emotions, and imaginations to create captivating and innovative texts. AI, on the other hand, relies on pre-existing algorithms and models to generate suggestions and responses. It lacks the capacity for creative thinking and imagination that makes human beings unique.

In addition, AI struggles to understand the emotional subtleties and nuances of writing. Writing is a form of expression that allows authors to convey emotions and create connections with readers. Chosen words, turns of phrase, metaphors, and descriptions help capture feelings and elicit emotional responses. AI can analyze existing texts and mimic certain patterns, but it struggles to grasp the essence of human emotions.

Another important aspect of human creativity and intuition is the ability to take risks and explore new ideas. Human authors can venture into uncharted territory, experiment with different narrative structures, and break established rules. AI, on the other hand, is limited by the data it is trained on. She struggles to think outside the box and come up with truly innovative ideas.

Despite these limitations, AI can still be a valuable tool for writers. It can help speed up the writing process by offering quick suggestions and helping with error correction. It can also be used as a source of inspiration to stimulate the creativity of authors. However, it is essential to recognize that AI cannot replace human creativity and intuition in writing.

Authors should keep in mind that AI is a tool, not a substitute for their own expertise and talent. They need to stay true to their artistic vision and use AI wisely, critically evaluating its suggestions and tailoring them to their specific needs. Additionally, human oversight is essential when using AI in writing, to ensure that the texts produced remain consistent, original, and emotionally engaging.

**Difficulty understanding context and nuances**

Artificial intelligence can sometimes have difficulty understanding the context and nuances of a text. Natural language processing algorithms used by AI can face obstacles when it comes to grasping the deeper meaning of a text or interpreting idioms, puns, or metaphors. As a result, AI can sometimes produce inappropriate results or misinterpret the author's intent. That's why authors need to remain vigilant and use judgment to evaluate AI suggestions.

When it comes to understanding the meaning of a text, contextual understanding is key. Human authors are able to grasp the subtleties of language and interpret words based on the overall context. They can understand the nuances, allusions, and cultural references that enrich the text. AI, on the other hand, relies on statistical models and algorithms that may lack this deep contextual understanding. It may rely on correspondences of words and sentences without fully grasping their meaning in the given context.

Another hurdle for artificial intelligence is the ability to interpret specific turns of phrase, language games, and pictorial comparisons. These linguistic elements bring color and depth to writing, but they can be difficult for AI to understand. Language-specific phrases, such as "putting water in your wine" or "having a cat down your throat," can seem strange or confusing to AI if it doesn't have a deep understanding of culture-specific customs and languages. Additionally, puns and metaphors may require some sensitivity and intuition to understand and use appropriately. AI may lack this ability to grasp the double meaning, subtlety, and irony that characterize these forms of expression.

Because of these limitations, AI can sometimes produce inappropriate or erroneous results. She can interpret a text literally that requires a more nuanced understanding. For example, if an author uses a metaphor to describe a situation, the AI could take that metaphor at face value and produce an incorrect interpretation. Similarly, AI may fail to grasp humor or irony in a text and offer suggestions that are lacking in the tone desired by the author.

However, this does not mean that AI is completely ineffective in understanding language. Recent advances in AI have led to significant improvements in AI's ability to understand and interpret human language. Pre-trained language models, such as ChatGPT, have shown promising results in generating text that approximates the quality of human writing. These models can take context into account and produce more accurate and appropriate responses.

So, it's important for authors to use their best judgment when using AI as a writing aid. They should evaluate the AI's suggestions keeping in mind its limitations and using their own judgment to refine and improve the text. AI can be a valuable way to generate ideas, improve grammar and sentence structure, but it cannot replace human understanding and intuition.

AI has made significant strides in understanding language, but it continues to face challenges when it comes to understanding the context and nuances of a text. Authors should keep in mind that AI is a tool that can provide useful suggestions, but it cannot replace their own contextual understanding and judgment. They must remain vigilant and exercise their judgment to evaluate the AI's suggestions and tailor them to their specific needs. By working collaboratively with AI, authors can harness the benefits of this technology while preserving their essential role as creators of unique and nuanced writing.

**Limitations in less common languages**

Limitation in less common languages is a topic of interest to many researchers and linguists. Less common languages are often overlooked in favor of more widely spoken languages such as English, Spanish, or French. However, these languages have unique peculiarities and challenges that deserve to be studied and understood.

One of the main limitations of less common languages is the availability of data. The most widely spoken languages tend to have abundant data, allowing researchers to train on more accurate language models. On the other hand, less common languages often have limited data, making it more difficult to create high-performance language models. This means that language models for less common languages are often less accurate and less efficient than those for more widely spoken languages.

Another limitation of less common languages is the size of their vocabulary. Languages that are more widely spoken tend to have a larger vocabulary, which allows for a greater variety of expressions and nuances of meaning. Less common languages, on the other hand, often have a smaller vocabulary, which can make it more difficult to express certain ideas or nuances of meaning. This can make it more difficult to translate automatically between languages. as it is often necessary to use borrowed phrases or words to express specific concepts.

Grammatical complexity is another limitation of less common languages. The most widely spoken languages tend to have more standardized and simpler grammars, making it easier to understand and produce the language. Less common languages, on the other hand, may have more complex and varied grammars, which can make it more difficult to understand and produce the language. For example, some African languages have complex verb conjugation systems that can make it difficult to produce the language.

The limitation of less common languages is also linked to the availability of teaching resources and materials. The most widely spoken languages tend to have more learning resources and teaching materials, making it easier to learn and master the language. Less common languages, on the other hand, often have fewer learning resources and teaching materials, which can make it more difficult to learn and master the language.

Finally, the limitation of less common languages is also related to the perception and value given to these languages. The most widely spoken languages are often seen as more important and useful, while less common languages are often seen as less important and useful. This can lead to less consideration and appreciation of less common languages, which can limit their development and teaching.

Despite these limitations, it is important to emphasize the importance of less common languages. These languages have unique peculiarities and cultural richness that deserve to be studied and understood. In addition, learning and mastering less common languages can open new doors and opportunities, both personally and professionally.

To promote learning and mastery of less common languages, it is important to develop appropriate learning resources and teaching materials. Researchers and teachers can work together to create effective teaching materials and learning tools for less common languages. In addition, it is important to raise awareness and promote the value of less common languages, highlighting their cultural importance and potential for personal and professional development.

In sum, the limitation of less common languages is a significant challenge for researchers, teachers and learners. They have unique peculiarities and challenges that deserve to be studied and understood. By developing appropriate learning resources and teaching materials, and by raising awareness and valuing less common languages, we can promote the learning and mastery of these languages, and thus contribute to the linguistic and cultural diversity of our world.

**Need for human oversight**

Despite the benefits it offers, AI still needs human oversight to ensure the quality and authenticity of writings.

AI-based writing tools are designed to analyze and understand textual content. They use sophisticated algorithms to offer suggestions for improvement, correct grammatical errors, and sometimes even generate original content. These features can be very useful for authors, providing them with ideas, corrections, and tips to polish their work.

However, it's important to remember that AI is not foolproof. AI models used in writing tools are trained on large data sets, but they can still produce incorrect or inappropriate results. This is especially true when it comes to sensitive or complex topics that require in-depth and nuanced understanding.

AI-based writing tools may lack discernment in the tone or intent of a text. They may offer suggestions that don't match the author's original intent or aren't tailored to the specific context. For example, in the case of a sensitive topic like politics, AI can suggest phrases or ideas that don't fit the author's perspective or can be perceived as biased.

That's why it's critical that authors don't blindly rely on AI's suggestions. Human monitoring is necessary to evaluate and filter the suggestions offered by the AI. Authors should exercise their critical judgment and decide which suggestions are appropriate and in line with their creative intent. They also need to remain aware of the limitations of AI and not lose sight of their own expertise and artistic vision.

In addition, human intervention is crucial to ensure the authenticity of the writings. AI can be used to generate original content, but it is important that this aspect is clearly stated and that the author takes responsibility for that content. Transparency is essential to maintain the integrity of the writing and avoid any confusion or misunderstandings.

It is also essential to have human oversight to spot harmful directions that could manifest in artificial intelligence models. Since AI is trained with already existing data, it can unintentionally reflect the biases and preconceptions present in that data. Thus, it is crucial to conduct continuous verification of the AI's performance to ensure that it does not inadvertently create stereotypes or discrimination.

AI still needs human oversight to ensure the quality and authenticity of writings. AI-based writing tools can produce incorrect or inappropriate results, especially when it comes to sensitive or complex topics. Authors should therefore exercise caution and not blindly rely on AI's suggestions. Human intervention and evaluation remain essential to preserve artistic integrity and ensure quality writing. By cultivating a balanced approach between AI and human expertise, authors can make the most of AI-powered writing tools while preserving their unique voice and creative vision.

## The Ethics of Using AI in Writing

The use of artificial intelligence in the field of writing has opened up new perspectives for authors, but it also raises important ethical questions. When using AI algorithms in the writing process, it is crucial to consider the issues related to cultural and social biases that may be present in the datasets used to train these algorithms.

The algorithms used by AI are typically trained on large existing data sets, which may reflect cultural or social biases. These biases can manifest themselves in the suggestions or results produced by the AI, thus influencing the content of the texts generated. For example, if the dataset used to train AI is mostly text from a specific culture, this can result in suggestions or results that reflect and perpetuate stereotypes or biases of that culture.

So, it's crucial to take these considerations into account and critically evaluate when using AI in writing. Authors should be aware of the limitations of AI and the potential biases that may be present in the results generated. They need to exercise their critical judgment and decide if the AI's suggestions align with their ethical values and creative intent.

## The issue of intellectual property

The issue of intellectual property in the context of AI is a complex and controversial topic that raises important ethical questions about creation, ownership, and responsibility. With the increasing use of AI for content creation, the issue of intellectual property has become more relevant than ever.

Intellectual property refers to the legal ownership of creations of the human mind, such as ideas, discoveries, inventions, literary and artistic works, and symbols. It is protected by laws and international treaties that guarantee creators the right to be recognized as the authors of their works and to collect royalties.

However, the issue of intellectual property for works created by AI is more complex. Who is the owner of these works? Is it the person who created the AI model, or is it the machine itself?

Some argue that the person who created the AI model is the owner of all the works created by that model. According to them, the creation of a literary or artistic work is a creative process that involves human skills, knowledge, and decisions. Therefore, this person is considered the owner of the work.

However, others argue that the machine itself is the owner of the work, as it is the machine that created the work using its own algorithms and data. According to this view, the machine is seen as an author as the creator of the work.

There are also arguments in favour of a third option: common intellectual property. According to this vision, works created by AI should be considered as collective creations, the result of collaboration between humans and machines. In this case, intellectual property would be shared between human creators and machines.

The issue of intellectual property for works created by AI also raises questions about legal and professional liability. If a work created by AI violates any copyright or ethical standards, who is responsible? Is it the person who created the AI model, or is it the machine itself?

In addition, the issue of intellectual property for AI-created works also raises questions about transparency and trust. If a text is created by a machine, does the reader have the right to know who the creator of the work is? Transparency is key to ensuring the trust and trustworthiness of works created by AI.

Finally, the issue of intellectual property for AI-created works also raises questions about the future of creation and intellectual property. If machines can create high-quality literary and artistic works, what will be the roles of humans in creating the future? The answer to this question is complex, as it raises questions about the future of creation, intellectual property and accountability.

In sum, the issue of intellectual property for AI-created works is complex and raises important ethical questions about creation, ownership, accountability, and transparency. It is important to find answers to these questions to ensure that creation and intellectual property are protected and respected in the age of AI.

**The issue of transparency**

The issue of transparency and ethics in writing a novel with the help of artificial intelligence (AI) has become central to the debate about the future of creative writing. As technology advances, allowing AI to play an increasingly active role in the creative process, the need to address these issues from an ethical perspective becomes imperative. Transparency is not only about the disclosure of the use of AI, but also encompasses the wider implications of this practice on the relationship between the author, the work, and the reader.

In this context, transparency refers to the clarity and honesty with which authors reveal the contribution of AI in the creation of their works. This demand for transparency goes beyond mere professional courtesy; It touches on the integrity of the literary work itself and the trust that the reader places in the author. A lack of transparency can not only erode that trust, but also raise questions about the authenticity of creative expression and the value of the literary work in an era where technology is ubiquitous.

Ethics, in this framework, refers to the moral responsibility of the author in managing this triangular relationship between the human, the machine, and the literary product. Authors should ask themselves how much credit they are willing to share the credit for their creation with a non-human entity. This ethical questioning is not limited to a simple practical consideration but touches on deeper questions about the nature of creativity and the role of the human in the act of creation.

The issue of fairness to authors who choose not to use AI in their creative process is also an important ethical consideration. Transparency in the use of AI ensures a balanced playing field, where works are evaluated and valued not only for their literary merit, but also for the integrity of their creative process. This preserves the value of human labor in a field that is increasingly influenced by technology.

Finally, the impact of using AI on the reader cannot be ignored. Transparency allows readers to fully understand what they are reading and where it is coming from, providing them with the opportunity to make informed choices about the works they support. This honesty strengthens the relationship between author and reader, based on trust and mutual respect.

However, the use of AI in writing should not be dismissed solely because of these ethical concerns. Rather, it's important to strike a balance between the benefits AI can offer and the need to mitigate bias. Authors can collaborate with AI experts and ethicists to develop AI-based writing tools that consider these ethical issues and are designed to promote diversity, inclusion, and equity in the writing process.

In addition, it is essential to have transparency and accountability mechanisms in place to ensure that AI results in writing are critically examined. Authors should be aware of how the AI has been trained and the potential biases that may arise from it. They should also be willing to step in and adjust AI suggestions to ensure that the final content reflects their own values and intentions.

Finally, it's important to recognize that AI isn't a magic bullet for solving all writing problems. While it can offer valuable suggestions and improvements, it cannot replace human creativity and talent. Authors must continue to develop their skills and cultivate their unique voice, using AI as a complementary tool rather than a substitute.

# Chapter 3

# Creating Inspirational Prompts for Writing

## Techniques and Tips for Designing Prompts That Stimulate the Imagination

Artificial intelligence is transforming the world at breakneck speed, opening up new avenues in many fields, from medicine to art, and far beyond. At the heart of this revolution is a seemingly simple, but profoundly significant concept: prompt. A prompt, in the context of AI, is an instruction or input of data provided to an AI system to elicit a specific response or outcome. This definition, while concise, hides the complexity and power inherent in prompts in human interaction with intelligent machines.

The role of prompts extends far beyond simply providing inputs to an AI system. They also act as catalysts for innovation and creativity in the development of AI. By asking open-ended questions or presenting specific challenges in the form of prompts, researchers and developers can push AI systems to explore new and unconventional solutions. This approach is fundamental in areas such as solving complex problems, generating creative content, and improving user-machine interactions.

Using prompts effectively requires a nuanced understanding of how AI interprets and processes information. This means not only choosing words carefully, but also structuring prompts in a way that guides the AI to the type of response or action they want. For example, in text generation, a well-designed prompt can encourage an AI model to produce more creative, consistent, and contextually appropriate writing.

Similarly, in machine learning applications, precisely worded prompts can improve the accuracy and efficiency of model training.

The ability to create inspiring and effective prompts is therefore a valuable skill in today's technological landscape. It requires a deep understanding of both the relevant AI technology and the specific application area. For educators, this means incorporating guidelines into the curriculum to cultivate critical thinking and problem-solving skills in students.  For professionals and businesses, this means using prompts to optimize processes, innovate products and services, and improve customer engagement.

# What is a prompt?

The notion of "prompt" occupies a central place, acting as the bridge between the human and the machine. A prompt, in this advanced technological framework, is essentially an instruction or series of instructions specifically formulated and addressed to an artificial intelligence system. This interaction can take a variety of forms, ranging from simple questions to complex guidelines, each serving as a catalyst to actuate or guide the AI's response. Just as a conductor guides his musicians, a prompt guides the AI, telling it the path to follow, the nature of the task at hand, or the expected response.

Although the French translation of "prompt" is usually "invite", I have deliberately opted for the use of the term "prompt" in this book. This decision is based on the fact that Artificial Intelligence better understands the meaning of the word "prompt" as an instruction explicitly directed at it, as opposed to "prompt", which could be perceived as a simple proposal or a form of politeness. Indeed, "prompt" takes on a more directive character in this context, thus facilitating communication between the user and the AI.

On the other hand, it is crucial to note that the choice of the term "prompt" actively participates in clarifying the user's intentions with regard to the AI, thus avoiding ambiguities and other misunderstandings that can harm the creative process. Indeed, by adopting a more affirmative and categorical vocabulary, the author clearly manifests his expectations and objectives, guiding the AI in the performance of specific tasks and promoting the achievement of satisfactory results.

To consider a prompt, it is essential to recognize its dual nature: it is both question and order, request and direction. As a robust tool, when used properly, a prompt can unlock the impressive potential of AI, enabling elaborate interactions and responses tailored to the user's specific needs. Take, for example, a simplistic prompt like "What's the weather today?" where the AI is asked to provide a weather update. Or a more complex prompt, such as "Develop a marketing plan for an innovative product," which tasks the AI with designing a complete strategy based on the established parameters.

Indeed, a skillfully composed prompt has the remarkable ability to mobilize all the functions of AI, thus amplifying efficiency and productivity during the creative process. By understanding how to cleverly manipulate a prompt, you can transcend the conventional boundaries of human-computer interaction and usher in an era of collaborative and resourceful collaboration. So, don't be afraid to experiment and optimize your prompts for more personalized and impactful results. Don't underestimate the power of these modest strings, as they are the key to synchronization between humans and artificial intelligence.

The versatility of prompts is another crucial aspect of their usefulness in AI. They can vary greatly in complexity and specificity, ranging from general queries to detailed instructions. This flexibility allows users to tailor their communication with AI to achieve a variety of goals, whether it's gaining insights, solving complex problems, or generating creative content. The ability of a prompt to encapsulate a request or instruction largely determines the relevance and accuracy of the AI's response. Thus, formulating a prompt is an art in itself, requiring clarity, precision, and an understanding of how AI works.

In the context of machine learning and advanced AI systems, prompts are not simply commands, but triggers of cognitive processes in the machine's artificial mind. Each prompt is an opportunity for AI to analyze, process, and respond appropriately, using its extensive databases and algorithmic capabilities. The way a prompt is worded can significantly influence the type and quality of the response. A clear and well-defined prompt usually leads to more accurate results, while a vague or ambiguous prompt can lead to less targeted or even erroneous responses.

In addition, the strategic use of AI prompts opens up opportunities for personalization and adaptation. By modifying the structure and content of a prompt, users can guide the AI to respond in a way that is more tailored to their specific needs or contexts. This is especially relevant in areas such as customer service, where well-designed prompts can lead to more natural and efficient interactions between customers and AI systems.

In addition, AI prompts play a crucial educational role. In learning environments, for example, carefully crafted prompts can encourage AI to provide detailed explanations, guide users through complex concepts, or come up with creative solutions to problems. This makes AI not only a response tool, but also an active partner in the learning and discovery process.

Prompts act as keys to endless possibilities. They are the instrument through which users communicate their wants and needs to AI, triggering thought and action processes within these sophisticated systems. The ability to formulate effective prompts is therefore an essential skill for any user wishing to make the most of artificial intelligence, whether for everyday tasks, professional challenges, or creative explorations. By understanding and mastering the art of prompting, we can not only improve our interaction with AI, but also open up new horizons in how we use technology to enrich our lives.

# Tips for Writing Effective Prompts

The key to writing effective prompts is to start with a clear understanding of the intended purpose. A prompt should be designed with a specific intention, whether it's to get specific information, generate creative ideas, or lead to deep thinking. For this, it is crucial to be specific and direct in your formulation. Avoid ambiguities and be as descriptive as possible to clearly guide the expected response. For example, if you're looking to generate ideas for a story, indicate the genre, setting, and key elements you want to include. This specificity makes it possible to obtain more targeted and relevant responses, thus increasing the effectiveness of the prompt.

## An efficient prompt

To build an effective prompt, it is essential to adhere to a logical and consistent structure. Follow these tips to optimize your prompts and maximize their potential:

**Clear context and purpose:** Start by briefly explaining the context of what you want to accomplish and the purpose of the prompt.

**Specific instructions:** Provide clear instructions on what you want from the model. This can include details about the type of response you want to get, the specific items you want to include, and more.

**Examples (if necessary):** If possible, give examples to illustrate what you want from the model. This can help clarify your expectations and guide the generation of the response.

**Quality guidelines:** If you have specific quality criteria or important things to consider, be sure to mention them in the prompt.

**Encouraging creativity:** If you want to encourage the creativity of the model, feel free to mention it in the prompt. This can prompt the model to explore different approaches to meet your demand.

Here's an example of a prompt to create a short story:

"You're going to create a short story themed around the fantasy adventure (Clear Context and Purpose). Write a story of about 200 words that features a young explorer who discovers a mysterious door hidden in the heart of an enchanted forest. Explore the challenges he faces as he walks through this door and describe the wonders of the fantasy world that opens up to him on the other side (Precise instructions). You can include examples of challenges such as magical creatures, puzzles to solve, strange landscapes, etc. (Examples). Make sure the story is well-structured, with a clear beginning, middle, and end. Make sure the descriptions are lively and captivating to immerse the reader in the adventure (Quality Guidelines). Feel free to be imaginative and introduce unique fantasy elements to make the story memorable and surprising (Encouragement of creativity)."

While it may seem like a lot of work to write every prompt, it's well worth the effort, as well-designed prompts lead to much higher quality results. Online, you'll discover a wide range of pre-built prompts that can be adapted to your novelistic needs, as well as a wealth of resources on the Ai BEYOND THE PEN website, which I'll introduce you to later in this book.

 In the meantime, here's the story the AI came up with based on the previously written prompt:

*In the heart of a forest where every tree whispered ancient secrets, Eliott, the young explorer, stumbled over a strangely carved root. Following the whispers to a clearing, he discovered a door adorned with glittering runes, guarded by an old oak tree with intertwined branches.*

*Driven by curiosity, Eliott crosses the threshold, his senses immediately assailed by the magic of the world behind the door. Waterfalls of unknown colors fell into an inverted sky, and crystal-winged creatures sang in a language of light.*

*But every wonder came with a challenge. To advance, he had to solve riddles posed by silver sphinxes, whose questions were woven of ancient wisdom and celestial riddles. When he failed, the paths changed, forcing him to learn from his mistakes and adapt.*

*Eventually, Eliott came to a shimmering lake where the truth was revealed to him: every trial was a lesson, every creature a guide, and the enchanted forest a reflection of his adventurous soul. With a transformed heart and newly acquired wisdom, he returned home, the door slowly closing, now an eternal part of his legend.*

This prompt format is ideal for composing larger texts. On the other hand, when writing story segments, descriptions, or minor corrections, you won't need to resort to such a detailed prompt structure.

## Be challenging and provocative

Effective prompts are those that spark interest and stimulate the writer's creativity. Try to use intriguing words or phrases that capture the author's attention from the beginning. Avoid prompts that are too generic or predictable and could limit the imagination. Dare to be provocative and explore bold and original ideas.

Here are some examples of prompts:

*"Describe a chance encounter between a jewel thief and a private investigator, but give them unexpected motivations that challenge their traditional role."*

*"Imagine a world where dreams come true, but only for one day. Describe the daily lives of the locals and the unintended consequences of this donation. »*

*"Write a love letter from an inanimate object to its owner, expressing their feelings and unique perspective on their relationship."*

*"Create a dialogue between two strangers who meet in a blocked elevator. Use cryptic one-liners to create tension and mystery around their true identity. »*

*"Imagine a world where technology has advanced to the point where souvenirs can be bought and sold. Describe the story of a character who discovers that his memories have been manipulated without his knowledge. »*

*"Write a captivating action scene where the protagonist uses an everyday object in surprising ways to defend himself against a powerful enemy."*

> *"Create a story based on popular superstition but give it a scientific explanation that challenges traditional beliefs."*
>
> *"Imagine a world where animals have developed a form of communication with humans. Describe the story of a character who befriends an animal and the challenges they face in this relationship. »*

These prompts are designed to encourage you to think outside the box, explore bold ideas, and create compelling stories. Feel free to use them as a starting point for your own writing and let your creativity run wild!

**Offer Choices**

Give yourself the opportunity to choose between different themes or perspectives. This will help you customize the prompt and find an angle that better suits your style. For example, instead of saying, " *Write a story about a sea voyage* " you could suggest, "*Write a story about a sea voyage or a space adventure. »*

**Use tangible images or objects**

Recently, AI can now analyze images that are offered to it. This is the case, for example, with Dall-E, where AI can be asked to analyze an image. Using tangible images or objects can be extremely effective in sparking your imagination. Show a photo or give the AI a concrete object and ask it to write from that inspiration. This will help you see and interact with the prompt in a more realistic and immersive way.

As an example, I asked the AI to describe this image[2] :

---

[2] Created by DALL· E

*His posture is relaxed, one hand supporting his chin, the other resting on the bench.*

*The lake is calm with gentle ripples, reflecting the lush vegetation and diffuse light from a partly cloudy sky. The scene evokes a time of day when the light is soft, perhaps early in the morning or late afternoon.*

*The trees and plants that line the lake are varied, with bright green leaves, suggesting a sunny day. You can also see a few rocks on the surface of the water, near the shore.*

*The overall atmosphere of the image is calm and contemplative, inviting the viewer to stop and think, just as the boy does. Light and shadow are well-balanced, with areas illuminated by soft natural light and shadows that add depth to the scene. »*

PROMPT: Write me a short story based on the image that is displayed.

*"On the shores of a tranquil lake, where the waters reflect the changing sky like a mirror of the moods of the world, stands a wooden bench. It is on this bench that Remy likes to sit, far from the hustle and bustle of the city that always seems to be in a hurry, always noisy.*

*Remy has been coming here with his grandfather since he was a little boy. They come to feed the ducks, throw rocks to create endless ricochets, and talk about anything and everything. But most of all, they come for the stories. His grandfather, a born storyteller, populated the lake with fantastic creatures and ancestral legends. Every ripple was the passing of a mermaid, every rustle of the wind in the leaves, the breath of a hidden dragon.*

*Today, Remy is sitting alone for the first time. His grandfather left him his most precious legacy – a boundless imagination and a world of wonders at his fingertips.*

*Remy closes his eyes and listens: the lake whispers new stories to him. He can hear his grandfather's laughter in the lapping of the water, see the silhouettes of fairy tales in the clouds.*

*So he opens his little notebook, the same one in which his grandfather drew maps of imaginary worlds, and starts doodling. With every word, every drawing, he feels his grandfather next to him, guiding his hand. Remy knows he's not really alone – as long as he keeps the stories alive, so will his grandfather, by his side, on that wooden bench in front of this eternal lake. »*

With AI, you could come up with ideas for stories, characters, locations, or feelings that can help you create a new story or enhance the one you're writing.

**Ask provocative questions**

Provocative questions are a great way to create prompts that prompt people to think and explore new ideas. Formulate questions that question existing beliefs or habits, or that invite you to think about moral or ethical issues. This will inspire you to go beyond the obvious answers and dig deeper to find answers.

Here are a few examples:

*"Imagine a world where lying is considered a virtue and truth is considered a crime. Describe how this affects human relationships and society as a whole. »*

*"Write a story where humans discover that they are actually artificial creations and that their entire existence has been programmed. How do they react to this revelation? »*

*"You wake up one morning to find that you can read other people's minds. How does this change your perception of reality and how do you adapt to this new ability? »*

*"Imagine a world where machines have taken over society and humans are reduced to mere utilitarian objects. Tell the story of a human trying to rebel against this technological domination. »*

*"Describe a society where love is considered a disease and is strictly forbidden. How do two people manage to love each other despite this prohibition and what are the consequences? »*

**Encourage Emotional Engagement**

Prompts that elicit strong emotions are often the most powerful. Try to use words or situations that evoke intense emotions, whether it's joy, sadness, fear, or love. When you're emotionally invested in the topic, it reflects in your writing and makes the story more captivating.

*"Describe a moment when a character makes a difficult decision that turns their life upside down, with an emphasis on the intense emotions they are feeling at that moment."*

*"Imagine a character dealing with the loss of a loved one and describe their grieving process, exploring the complex emotions and stages they go through to find healing."*

*"Write a passionate love scene between two characters, describing the burning emotions and physical sensations that overwhelm them."*

*"Create a story that explores feelings of betrayal, where a character discovers that someone they trusted completely has betrayed them. Detail the emotions of anger, sadness, and confusion that emerge from this situation. »*

*"Imagine a main character faced with a difficult moral choice, where he has to face an ethical dilemma. Describe the internal struggles and conflicting emotions they feel as they struggle with this decision. »*

**Provide Creative Constraints**

Creative constraints can be an effective way to boost your creativity. For example, you can challenge yourself to write a story using only dialogue, or to create a poem using only words starting with a certain letter. Creative constraints force you to think innovatively and step out of your comfort zone.

*"Create a poem or song using only single-syllable words. Constrained by this language limitation, explore how you can express complex emotions and evocative images. »*

*"Imagine a story where dialogue between characters is limited to sentences of no more than three words. How can you create intriguing tensions, relationships, and twists despite this communication constraint? »*

*"Describe a thrilling action scene that takes place exclusively in total darkness. How do you use the other senses of the characters to create a tense and immersive atmosphere? »*

*"Write a children's story using only words that start with the same letter, for example, all words start with the letter 'P'. How can you tell a compelling story while respecting this linguistic constraint? »*

# Find the right prompts for your purpose

Whether your goal is to explore the intricate depths of human emotions, build fantastical worlds, or unravel captivating plots, choosing the right prompt is essential.

The art of choosing suitable prompts is fundamental for any writer looking to express their creative aspirations and stimulate their imagination in a productive way. Recognizing those that align with your unique artistic vision is key to unlocking the full potential of your story. Each writer, with his distinctive voice, will find in certain prompts a particular echo of his ideas and ambitions. Selecting these catalysts wisely can transform a simple idea into a profound and captivating work.

## Understanding Your Writing Goal

Before choosing a prompt, it's essential to have a clear understanding of your writing purpose. Whether you want to write an informative article, a fictional story, or a persuasive essay, your choice of prompt will be influenced by this goal. You have to know who you're talking to: who is the readership of your work? This is essential for adapting your writing. For example, the style required for children is not the same as for an adult or professional audience.

**Choose relevant prompts**

Once you've identified your writing goal, look for prompts that are relevant to what you want to accomplish.

For example, if you're writing an article about health, choose prompts that encourage you to explore topics related to health and wellness. Here are some examples of prompts:

**Quick to explore the benefits of meditation with a focus on concrete approaches and personal testimonies:**

*"Write an article about the mental health benefits of meditation, with a focus on specific techniques and personal testimonials."*

**Prompt intended to provide useful and accessible information on how to maintain a balanced diet, with an emphasis on simplicity and practicality:**

*"Write a beginner's guide to a balanced diet, including practical tips for incorporating healthy food choices into daily life."*

**Quick to present feasible exercise options to those with limited free time, with an emphasis on efficiency and flexibility:**

*"Describe an exercise routine that is appropriate for people with busy schedules, highlighting how to incorporate physical activity into a busy daily routine."*

**Prompt aimed at raising awareness of the critical importance of sleep and offering strategies to improve sleep quality.**

*"Write a detailed article on the importance of sleep for overall health, including tips for improving sleep quality."*


**Explore the impact of stress on health and provide research-based advice to manage it effectively.**

*"Present an analysis of the latest research on the effects of stress on physical health, and propose proven methods to manage and reduce stress."*

# Chapter 4

# Inspiring prompts for characters

## Create Engaging Dialogues and Scenarios

Artificial intelligence can be a valuable partner in the writing of your book, especially for character development. Imagine a tool that not only generates initial character ideas but also helps you dig deeper into their profile. AI can offer you rich descriptions, complex personality traits, and even family history or personal histories. You can start with these suggestions and build on them to create unique characters.

One fascinating aspect of using AI in writing is its ability to simulate dialogue. By capturing the tone and voice of your characters, the AI can generate realistic exchanges, giving you insight into their interaction and helping you polish the dialogue. This feature is especially useful for checking the consistency of character voices across different scenes.

AI can also help structure your scenes. By providing context and directions, the AI can create sketches of scenes that you can then expand. This can be especially useful for overcoming writer's block or for exploring different narrative directions.

Another advantage of AI is its ability to maintain character consistency. By analyzing your manuscript, the AI can identify inconsistencies in behavior or dialogue, helping you keep a clear guideline for each character. In addition, the AI can suggest ways to develop your characters based on the story arc, coming up with ideas to introduce conflicts, challenges, or evolutions.

Finally, if your book is aimed at an international audience, AI can help you adapt your characters to different cultures. This cultural sensitivity is crucial to creating characters that resonate with a wide range of readers.

Using AI in book writing is an exciting adventure. Tools like OpenAI's ChatGPT, online character generators, or writing software with built-in AI features can be explored to enrich your characters and enhance your creative process. Each tool offers its own benefits and combining them can open new doors in the field of creative writing.

Here are five prompts that can help you discover and explore characters for your writing:

**Historical Inspiration Prompt** : *"Imagine a character who lives in an important historical period. How does this era influence his choices, beliefs, and relationships? Describe a typical day in his life, with an emphasis on historical and cultural details. »*

**Inner Conflict Prompt** : *"Create a character who struggles with a major inner conflict, such as a moral dilemma or deep fear. How does this conflict influence his interactions with others and the decisions he makes? "*

**Transformation Prompt** : *"Develop the story of a character who undergoes a significant transformation. What triggering event causes this change, and how does the character evolve through the story? "*

**Complex Relationships Prompt** : *"Imagine a character whose relationships with people close to you are complex and nuanced. How do these relationships affect his behavior and worldview? Give specific examples of relationship dynamics. "*

**Personal Quest Prompt** : *"Write about a character in search of something meaningful, whether it's a personal purpose, a hidden truth, or a meaning in life. How does this quest lead him to discoveries about himself and the world around him? "*

Each of these prompts is designed to spark your creativity and help you explore different facets and depths of your characters. By responding to these prompts, you can unveil unique and interesting aspects of the characters you create for your writing.

To see more ideas for character creation prompts, go to the laplumedigitale.com website

## Character creation

Artificial intelligence can be a remarkable tool for character creation and can inspire you with unique ideas and characteristics for your characters, such as their personality traits, appearance, personal history, and motivations. This can be especially useful when you're looking for new ideas or want to explore different directions for your character development.

In addition, AI can help you build detailed profiles for each character. It can incorporate things like the characters' backgrounds, relationships, goals, and conflicts they might face. This approach helps to create more complex and realistic characters, enriching the story of your novel.

AI can also assist you in creating dialogue and interactions between characters. It can offer lines of dialogue or suggest how different characters might interact with each other. This can be especially helpful for overcoming writer's block or for adding depth to character dynamics.

Finally, the use of AI in the character creation process can not only make your job as a writer easier, but also open doors to unprecedented creativity and innovation. By harnessing the power of AI, you can explore new avenues in the development of your novel and bring captivating and memorable characters to life.

## Creating Character Profiles with AI

The integration of artificial intelligence (AI) into the creation of novel characters opens up fascinating possibilities for authors. AI, with its advanced analytics and data generation capabilities, can significantly assist in the development of detailed character profiles. By providing suggestions for character traits, personal backgrounds, and even motivations, AI allows writers to explore new creative avenues.

AI algorithms can generate innovative ideas for characters, drawing inspiration from vast literary databases. This approach creates characters with unique personality traits, rich personal stories, and complex motivations. For example, an author can enter basic characteristics like a character's age or cultural background, and the AI can then come up with more detailed developments, such as past relationships that shaped the character's personality.

One of the most notable benefits of AI in character creation is its ability to make characters more realistic and nuanced. Algorithms can analyze patterns of human behavior to provide suggestions on how characters might react in different situations, enriching their emotional and psychological depth.

In addition, AI can be of great help in developing relationships between characters. By understanding the intricacies of human interactions, she can suggest complex and believable relationship dynamics between characters, based on their personality traits and past experiences. This is especially useful for creating realistic and captivating interactions in the narrative.

AI also adapts to different literary genres and styles. Whether one is writing a sci-fi novel, a historical drama, or a contemporary romance, the AI can adjust its suggestions to align with the tone and context of the narrative. This flexibility is a great asset for writers who want to explore different genres.

Here are some prompt examples to help you with character profile creation. Feel free to add details that relate to your novel or specifying the gender or age of the character. You can also start with a generic prompt and, depending on the answers, ask for more details or depths.  For more prompt ideas, I invite you to visit the website aidigitalpen.com

**Character Origins** : *"Describe a character who comes from a unique or unexpected cultural background, and explains how their heritage influences their perspectives and interactions with others."*

**Conflicting personality traits** : *"Imagine a character who combines a typically positive personality trait with a negative trait, for example, someone who is very empathetic, but also extremely manipulative."*

**Character Evolution** : *"Creates a character who undergoes a major transformation due to a key event in their life. What is this event and how does it change his behavior and beliefs? "*

**Relationships and dynamics**: *"Designs a character by focusing on their relationships with others. How do these relationships shape their identity and decisions? "*

**Internal conflicts**: *"Think of a character who is torn between two difficult moral choices or conflicting desires. How does this internal conflict manifest itself in his behavior? »*

**Secrets and Revelations**: *"Invent a character who hides an important secret. How does this secrecy affect his interactions and choices? What happens when the secret is finally revealed? "*

**Strengths and Weaknesses**: *"Describe a character by emphasizing their greatest strengths and weaknesses. How do these traits influence his journey through history? "*

**Ambitions and fears**: *"Imagine a character with a specific ambition and deep fear. How do these two aspects influence his quest or journey in the narrative? "*

**Legacy and Heirs**: *"Creates a character who has to deal with a heavy legacy, be it financial, family, or cultural. How does this affect his life and relationships? "*

**A Radical Change**: *"Think of a character who radically changes their perspective or lifestyle because of an experience or encounter. What triggers this change and what are the consequences? "*

## AI Character Customization

Artificial intelligence can be a valuable tool to help you develop unique and authentic characters. AI can provide suggestions and patterns based on data analysis and sophisticated algorithms. This will allow you to explore different facets of their characters and delve deeper into their development.

For starters, you can provide the AI with basic information about the character, such as their physical appearance, history, character traits, and motivations. AI can then generate additional insights based on this information. For example, it may suggest specific personality traits, family history, or past experiences that could influence the character's behavior.

AI can also help create authentic dialogue by studying the language and expressions of different types of characters. By analyzing sample dialogue, the AI can suggest appropriate lines that match the character's personality and identity.

Additionally, AI can be used to explore characters' motivations and emotional reactions. By analyzing patterns of human behavior, she can provide suggestions on how a character might react in certain situations, based on their personality and story.

Here are some examples of suggestions you can use:

*"Describe a character who has a strange and inexplicable phobia. How does this phobia affect his interactions with the other characters and his path through the story? "*

*"Imagine a character who grew up in a very strict and conservative family environment. How has this upbringing shaped his personality and what are the consequences when this character finds himself confronted with different values and situations? "*

*"Create a character who has extraordinary talent in a specific area, but hides that talent for fear of failure or over attention. How does this character evolve as they explore and embrace this hidden talent? "*

*"Invent a character who is constantly in conflict with their beliefs and values. How does this character navigate moral dilemmas, and how do these internal conflicts influence their decisions and actions? "*

*"Imagine a character who has had a traumatic experience in the past. How did this experience shape his personality, relationships, and perception of the world? How does this character overcome the emotional scars of his past to find healing and redemption?"*

## Character Relationship Development

AI can analyze interactions between characters by studying dialogue, actions, and emotions expressed. By examining these interactions, she can detect tensions, moments of connection, and relationship patterns. Based on models of human relationships, AI can then provide you with suggestions to deepen those relationships.

For example, AI can identify key moments when characters could have gotten closer or farther away. It can suggest scenes or twists to intensify emotions and conflicts between characters. In addition, it can also help you create moments of understanding and reconciliation, strengthening the bonds between the characters.

AI can also analyze characters' personality traits and motivations to better understand how these elements influence their interactions. She can suggest actions or dialogue that match each character's characteristics, which helps make their relationships more authentic and cohesive.

Additionally, AI can help you maintain consistency in relationships throughout your narrative. She can analyze the previous developments of each relationship and provide you with reminders or suggestions to avoid inconsistencies or oversights in the evolution of the interactions between the characters.

By using AI, you can benefit from an in-depth analysis of your characters' interactions, suggestions to deepen them and make them more realistic, as well as help to maintain relational consistency throughout your narrative.

Here are some examples of prompts you can use:

"Describe a chance encounter between two characters that provokes intense animosity from the start. Explore how this relationship can evolve over the course of the story and whether these characters can ultimately find common ground or mutual understanding. »

"Imagine a character who has betrayed another character in the past. Describe how this betrayal has affected their relationship and whether these characters can overcome their differences and rebuild trust. »

"Create an unlikely friendship between two characters from different backgrounds, with opposing interests, or contrasting personalities. Explore how this friendship develops and how it influences each of the characters in unexpected ways. »

"Invent a complex relationship between a mentor and his apprentice. Describe how these characters challenge, inspire, and support each other throughout their journey, highlighting the ups and downs of their relationship. »

"Imagine a tumultuous family relationship between two characters, such as rival siblings or a conflicted parent-child relationship. Explore how these blood ties can be put to the test and how characters can ultimately find the reconciliation or distance needed to evolve. »

## Conflicts and character development

AI can play a vital role in your novel for conflict and character development. It can help you in a number of ways.

First, the AI can analyze interactions and dialogues between characters to detect potential conflicts. She can spot moments of tension, disagreement, or differences of opinion, and suggest ways to escalate them. In this way, AI can help make conflicts more dynamic and captivating for your readers.

Additionally, by examining the characters' actions and decisions, AI can help you develop their evolution. It can identify key moments when a character faces challenges or dilemmas, which can lead to transformation or growth. AI can provide you with ways to describe these changes realistically and meaningfully.

By using character development models, AI can also help you create compelling story arcs. It can analyze your characters' personality traits, motivations, and goals, and suggest situations or challenges that push them to evolve. AI can help you define the stages of their journey, from initial conflict to final resolution or transformation.

In addition, AI can help you maintain consistency and progression of conflict and character evolution throughout your novel. By analyzing previous developments, it can provide you with reminders or suggestions to avoid inconsistencies or backtracking.

However, it's important to note that AI is a tool that provides you with suggestions and analysis. As an author, you have the power to make the final decisions about conflicts and the evolution of your characters. Trust your instincts and creative vision to bring captivating conflicts and ever-changing characters to life.

Here are some prompt templates you can leverage:

"Describe a character who finds himself facing a heartbreaking moral dilemma. How does this internal conflict affect his actions and personal growth? Explore how this character makes difficult decisions and how this shapes their evolution. »


"Imagine two characters who have conflicting goals. Describe how these opposing goals create conflict and tension between them. How do these characters evolve when faced with choices that challenge their priorities? »


"Create a character who has a deep fear of failure. Explore how this fear influences his actions and relationships with other characters. Describe how this character gradually overcomes this fear to achieve meaningful personal growth. »


"Invent an intense rivalry between two characters. Explore the reasons for this rivalry and how it evolves throughout the story. Describe how this rivalry pushes these characters to surpass themselves and redefine themselves as individuals. »


## Reinforce the authenticity and depth of the characters

AI can be a valuable tool to enhance the authenticity and depth of your characters. Through her analysis of patterns of human behavior and psychology, she can help you create more realistic and complex characters.


First, AI can help you develop your characters' personality traits consistently. By analyzing their actions, dialogues, and emotional reactions, it can provide you with insights into their habitual behavior. This allows you to create characters whose actions and choices are in line with their personality.

Additionally, AI can help you dig deeper into your characters' motivations and goals. She can analyze the circumstances and life experiences that have shaped their desires and aspirations. By understanding their underlying motivations, you can create characters whose actions are consistent with their motivations and whose goals are rooted in their past and values.

AI can also help you develop relationships between characters in an authentic way. By analyzing interactions and relationship dynamics, she can provide you with suggestions for creating realistic and emotionally rich connections. You can explore feelings, tensions, compromises, and changing relationships, creating deep connections between your characters.

The following suggestions provide examples of prompts to exploit:

*"Explore a character's past in detail: Delve into the memories and experiences that shaped your character. Describe a key event in their childhood or adolescence that had a significant impact on their personality and motivations. How is this reflected in his present actions and relationships? "*

*"Describe intense internal conflict: Create a moral or emotional dilemma for your main character. Explore the conflicting motivations that come into play and how it affects their decisions and personal growth. How does this challenge his identity and his core values?"*

*"Develop a complex and ambiguous relationship: Imagine two characters who have a relationship that oscillates between love and hate, friendship and betrayal. Describe moments of tension and mutual understanding, as well as moments of rupture and conflict. How does this ambivalent relationship shape the personalities and backgrounds of these characters? "*

*"Dive into a well-kept secret: Invent a secret buried deep in a character's life. Explore how this secret influences his interactions with other characters and how he perceives himself. How can this secret be revealed, and what will be the consequences for this character's trajectory? "*

*"Describe a moment of vulnerability: Put your main character in a situation where they are forced to reveal their deepest weaknesses and fears. How does this affect his relationship with the other characters and his personal evolution? How does he overcome this vulnerability and emerge transformed? "*

Chapter 5

# Use prompts to generate ideas

## Unleash your creativity

Prompts offer you an opportunity to think outside the box and explore new ideas. When using a prompt, let your imagination run wild and write down whatever comes to mind, without worrying about quality or consistency.

*"Imagine a world where dreams come true. Describe the life of a character who discovers this extraordinary ability and the unintended consequences of materializing their dreams. »*

## Explore different perspectives

Prompts can encourage you to see things from a different perspective. Try using a prompt to explore different perspectives on a given topic. This can help you develop a deeper understanding and broaden your worldview.

Here are some scenarios with suggested prompts for each:

**Describe a chance encounter in a coffee shop:**

*"Imagine that the person you are meeting is a time traveler who is desperate to return to the future. How does this affect the protagonist's life and what challenges does it pose to help them? »*

**Writing a story about an unsolved mystery:**

*"Add the constraint that the main protagonist is a ten-year-old child who is the only witness to the crime. How does the young protagonist solve the mystery using his innocence and insight? »*

**Imagining a world where dreams come true:**

Using the prompt: *"Add the constraint that each dream also comes true for another randomly chosen person from the world. How does this create complications and unintended consequences for the characters? »*

**Describe an epic adventure in a fantasy universe:**

*"Add in the constraint that the main protagonist is an anti-hero who hates conflict and prefers to stay out of trouble. How does this reluctant character find himself dragged into a perilous quest and how does this affect his personal development? »*

**Writing a story about the search for immortality:**

*"Add in the constraint that the main protagonist is a scientist who has discovered an elixir of immortality, but he must choose between his own immortality or that of his loved one.*

*How does this difficult decision push him to rethink his view of immortality, and what consequences does it lead to? »*

## Develop specific writing skills

Prompts can be designed in a way that helps you practice and reinforce specific skills, whether it's describing characters, creating gripping suspense, writing realistic dialogue, or building a detailed fantasy world.

By using prompts that emphasize these specific skills, you can practice developing and refining them. For example, if you want to improve your ability to describe places vividly, you can use a prompt that prompts you to describe an enchanting landscape or an abandoned place with all the appropriate sensory and emotional details.

Similarly, if you want to work on creating memorable characters, you can use a prompt that asks you to describe a character with their physical traits, personality, and unique backstory.

## Create Descriptions

Prompts can be used to develop your description skills

Choose a prompt that encourages you to describe a landscape, character, or scene in detail. Focus on using adjectives and metaphors to make your writing lively and captivating.

Describe the mountains stretching as far as the eye can see, their snow-capped peaks reflecting sunlight. Evoke the freshness of the air, the scents of wildflowers that fill the air. Accurately describe the shades of color: the bright green of the prairies, the deep blue of the shimmering lakes, the stark contrast between towering rocks and rushing waterfalls.

*The majestic mountains rise before you, stretching as far as the eye can see. Their snow-capped peaks glow in the golden rays of the sun, creating a dazzling spectacle. The light reflects off the pristine snow, creating ephemeral sparks that dance in the crystal-clear air.*

*The lakes, deep and serene blue, sparkle in the sun's rays. Their crystal-clear waters invite contemplation, offering perfect reflections of the majestic mountains that surround them. The contrasts are striking towering boulders emerge from the earth, forming powerful and intimidating structures. The waterfalls tumble down the rock walls with tumultuous force, creating a soothing murmur that mingles with the atmosphere. »*

## Define Novel Sections

A prompt can help define the sections of a novel by providing clear ideas and guidelines for structuring your story. It can be used to define the sections of the novel (Introduction, Initial Conflict, Plot Development, Climax, Resolution, and Conclusion).

*Introduction:*

*In this section, you can present the context of your story by describing a land that is overpopulated, depleted of its resources, and on the verge of collapse.*

*Initial Conflict:*

*In this section, you can introduce a conflict or obstacle that arises at the start of the trip to the moon. This could be a major technical failure of the space shuttle, an attempt at sabotage by groups opposed to the project, or even an unexpected threat from space.*

*Plot Development:*

*In this section, you can expand the plot by describing the life of the colonists on the Moon. You can explore the challenges they face, such as adapting to the lunar environment, managing limited resources, and building a functioning society.*

*Highlight:*

*In this section, you can reach the climax of the story, where tensions and conflicts come to a head. This can be a major crisis, such as a natural disaster on the Moon, internal conflicts within the colony, or even a confrontation with outside forces. This climax will put the fates of the main characters at stake and will have a significant impact on the fate of the lunar colony.*

*Resolution and Conclusion:*

*In this final section, you can describe how the characters overcome obstacles and achieve a resolution. This may involve personal sacrifices, surprising discoveries, or even revelations about the true motivations behind the exodus to the Moon. The conclusion can offer some form of resolution, while also leaving an opening for a possible continuation or exploration of another strand of the story. »*

Here are some other examples of Prompt:

*"A strange package is delivered to the protagonist's door. Inside is an enigmatic object that triggers a series of mysterious events. Describe how the protagonist investigates the origin of this object and uncovers a secret that could change his life forever. »*

*"Your main character wakes up in a completely different world, where the laws of physics are changed, and the rules of everyday life are turned upside down. Describe how the protagonist navigates this strange new world and must find a way home. »*

"Set in a dystopian future, your main character is chosen to participate in a deadly game where survival skills are put to the test. Describe his journey through this unforgiving arena and how he uses his wits and resources to evade his opponents and gain his freedom. »

"A character discovers an old notebook filled with notes and drawings, describing a legendary expedition to a mysterious island. Intrigued, the character decides to follow in the footsteps of this expedition and discover the hidden secrets of the island. Tell the story of his journey and the fascinating discoveries he makes along the way. »

"In a small, quiet town, strange things start to happen. The animals become aggressive, and the inhabitants mysteriously disappear. Your protagonist, a private investigator, is hired to solve this mystery. Describe how he follows clues, interrogates suspects, and uncovers a shocking truth that threatens the city's security. »

## Improving Storytelling

Prompts can also be used to improve your storytelling skills. Use suspense, character development, and dialogue techniques to make your narrative engaging.

Write a dialogue between Eric and Josée where they discuss a trip they want to take as a couple. But Josée doesn't want to go to Australia.

*Eric: Honey, I have a great idea for our next romantic trip. I've heard that Australia is amazing. What do you say?*

*Josée: Hmm, I'm not too sure I want to go to Australia, Eric. I mean, I'm sure it's a beautiful place, but I'm not really drawn to this destination. Could we consider something else?*

*Eric: Really? Australia has so much to offer. Breathtaking scenery, unique wildlife, white sand beaches and bustling cities. It would be an unforgettable experience for both of us.*

*Josée: I understand that Australia has its charms, but you know, I've always dreamed of visiting Europe. The old castles, the cobbled streets, the richness of history, it really fascinates me. Couldn't we consider a trip there?*

*Eric: Europe has an undeniable charm. But think of all the amazing scenery we could experience in Australia. Diving in the Great Barrier Reef, hiking in the Outback, not to mention the opportunity to see kangaroos and koalas in the wild.*

*Josée: I can't deny that it sounds fantastic, but Australia is also known for its dangerous wildlife. Venomous snakes and giant spiders scare me a little, I must admit. I'd prefer a place where I feel safer.*

*Eric: I understand your concerns. Safety is paramount. Perhaps we could consider a destination that combines both adventure and tranquility, such as Costa Rica or the Greek islands. These places offer beautiful nature, stunning beaches, and exciting activities without the risks associated with Australian wildlife.*

## Refine argumentation skills

If you want to develop your argumentation skills, choose prompts that require you to take a position on a given topic. Use strong arguments and persuasive evidence to support your point.

*"Do social networks have more positive or negative effects on modern society? Expand your argument by discussing pros such as global connection and spreading information, as well as cons such as cyberbullying and social media addiction. »*


*"Should education be made compulsory until the age of 18? Make a strong case by examining the benefits of ensuring a well-rounded education and addressing the possible economic and social disadvantages. »*


*"Are electric cars the ideal solution to fight climate change? Make your case by highlighting the benefits of reducing carbon emissions, but don't forget to also consider the challenges of charging infrastructure and battery production. »*


*"Should wild animals be kept in captivity in zoos? Present your argument by weighing the benefits of species education and conservation, as well as the disadvantages of deprivation of liberty and animal welfare. »*


*"Is remote work beneficial for employees and businesses? Expand your argument by addressing benefits such as flexibility and work-life balance, while also considering possible drawbacks such as difficulty maintaining productivity and collaboration. »*


These prompts will allow you to develop your argumentation skills by confronting you with a variety of topics and encouraging you to present solid and well-supported arguments. Feel free to engage in extensive research to support your point of view and consider different perspectives to hone your argumentation skills.

## Use Keywords

Keywords can also be used as prompts. Choose a keyword and write down everything that comes to mind related to that word. This can help you develop ideas and explore different aspects of a topic.

Use the following words as starting points to create a captivating story: clock, key, mystery, journey, fate.

*In the depths of an old town, hidden between the shadows of time, lies a mysterious clock. It is known to hold an unfathomable secret, a mystery that has captured people's imaginations for generations. An ancient key, passed down from generation to generation, is said to be the only one that can reveal the hidden truths of this enigmatic clock.*

*Our protagonist, a young adventurer named Alex, hears about this legend, and feels drawn to the call of mystery. He decides to embark on a perilous journey to find this mythical key and break through the Secrets of the Clock. His journey takes him through faraway lands and enchanting landscapes, where he encounters singular characters and surprising trials.*

*Some offer to help, while others seek to stop him, aware of the dangers that revealing the mystery of the clock could bring.*

As the journey progresses, Alex discovers enigmatic clues, scattered across ancient and mystical places. Each clue brings him closer to the coveted key and brings him closer to the truth hidden behind the clock. But he also realizes that his own destiny is intertwined with this quest, and that the discovery of the secret could change his life forever.

The tension builds as Alex gets closer to his final goal. The dark forces that watch over the mystery of the clock awaken and try to stop it. But with determination, courage and the help of his new allies, Alex overcomes the obstacles and finally reaches the legendary clock.

The long-sought-after key slips into the lock, and the clock starts moving. A complex mechanism is revealed, unleashing ancient knowledge and astonishing revelations. The mystery that has plagued minds for centuries is finally solved, and Alex understands the true power of this clock.

However, he also realizes that fate is a powerful and unpredictable force. The choices he has made throughout his journey have shaped his own story and have consequences that go beyond the simple mystery of the clock. Her journey has taught her that true treasure lies in self-discovery and acceptance of the destiny that lies ahead.

**Use Quotes**

Quotes can serve as prompts for brainstorming concepts and ideas. Choose a quote that speaks to you and write about what it means to you and how it can apply to your life or writing.

I want to reflect on this quote: "Creativity is intelligence having fun." - Albert Einstein

*For me, this quote resonates deeply. It evokes the idea that creativity is a form of intelligence that embraces play, curiosity, and exploration. It suggests that our ability to create, imagine, and innovate is an act of intelligence in itself, but also a source of pleasure and joy.*

*In my life, this quote reminds me of the importance of not taking creativity too seriously. Sometimes we can be too preoccupied with the pursuit of results or the pressure to produce something "perfect." But when I remember that creativity can be a form of play, it frees me from those rigid expectations. It allows me to explore, experiment, and have fun in the creative process.*

*All in all, this quote from Albert Einstein encourages me to approach creativity lightly, to play with ideas, to embrace my curiosity and to let my intelligence have fun in the creative process. Whether it's in my daily life or in my writing practice, I find inspiration in reminding myself that creativity is a form of intelligence that allows me to flourish and explore new horizons.*

## Character Development

Prompts can be used to develop characters by giving them situations, dilemmas, or challenges to overcome. By responding to a prompt, the writer can discover new facets of their characters and help them come to life on the page.

William is a shy and intelligent boy who has always been interested in auto mechanics. Describe in 1 sentence how the character lives his daily life, his interactions with others. Then, suggest a trigger in the character's life. Then give me some ideas in the character's journey.

*William, a shy and intelligent boy, leads a quiet and solitary life, spending most of his time studying auto mechanics and working in his workshop, often avoiding social interactions.*

*One day, while William was doing repairs in his workshop, he received an urgent call from a classmate's family. Their old car has broken down and they desperately need help fixing it. Hesitant but filled with empathy, William agrees to help.*

*This unexpected troubleshooting experience became a real turning point in William's life. While he successfully repairs the car and sees the gratitude and relief in the eyes of the family, he realizes how much his passion for auto mechanics can have a positive impact on the lives of others. This event encourages him to come out of his shell and consider how he could use his skills to help more people.*

*With this new perspective, William decided to start a car repair program for low-income families. He mobilizes his classmates and other mechanic enthusiasts to form a team dedicated to providing free repair services to those in need.*

*This journey led William to develop his leadership skills, connect with his community, and overcome his shyness to become a passionate advocate for equitable access to automotive services. His program became a resounding success, allowing many families to regain their mobility and independence.*

Using prompts in copywriting is an effective way to improve your writing skills, boost your creativity, and overcome writer's block. By finding prompts that fit your purpose, using prompts to generate ideas, developing specific writing skills, and experimenting with different types of prompts, you can enrich your writing and discover new perspectives.

# Chapter 6

# Artificial intelligence applications

## AI platforms under the microscope

The use of artificial intelligence is expanding and becoming ubiquitous in our daily lives, diversifying through different levels of complexity, application areas, and degrees of autonomy. Systems such as ChatGPT, QuillBot, Claude, and POE are among the most well-known examples of this technology.

Competition in the field of artificial intelligence has intensified, marking an era of unprecedented technological development. Tech giants such as Google, Microsoft, and Facebook are leading the charge, investing heavily in research and development to push the boundaries of what's possible with AI. Their goal is clear: to integrate AI into an ever-expanding range of products and services, transforming the way we live, work and interact.

However, AI innovation is not limited to the major players in the industry. A myriad of startups and small developers are also entering this race, proving that ingenuity and creativity know no size. Thanks to the increasing accessibility of AI development tools and platforms, almost anyone can now experiment and create custom AI solutions. This democratization of AI technology is driving a wave of innovation, where new applications and ideas are emerging at a rapid pace.

# My Favorite Apps

While I use many AIs for different needs, in this context I will focus on the ones that I primarily use that are best suited for writing novels with AI.

**ChatGPT** is an artificial language model developed by OpenAI, designed to understand and generate text in response to user requests. ChatGPT is capable of generating text that resembles that written by a human. It is based on deep learning and can perform a wide range of language-related tasks, such as text generation, translation, code writing, math problem solving, and more.

**QuillBot** is an AI-powered text rewriting tool that allows you to rephrase text with unlimited custom modes and 8 preset modes, such as *Standard, Fluency, Creative, and Academic*. You can also use the synonym slider to find the best synonym for any word or phrase and integrate QuillBot into Chrome and Microsoft Word. Although it can use multiple languages, it is very limited for the French language.

**CLAUDE** is a new generative artificial intelligence developed by Anthropic. It is considered a competitor to OpenAI's ChatGPT. Claude is able to answer natural language queries, generate summaries, write code, translate texts, search a document, discourse on a topic or solve mathematical problems. However, at the time of writing this book, Claude is not yet available directly to the general public and only available in certain countries.

**POE** is an app that promises access to different AI-based bots such as ChatGPT, Bard, or Bing Chat. Its creators intend to make it THE universal chat for generative AI, by making it easier for developers and users to create and use them. Poe stands out for its ability to ask questions simultaneously to multiple AIs.

In this book, I will focus on my two AIs that I use primarily in my novel writing process: ChatGPT and POE. Both platforms offer the ability to create custom AIs tailored to specific needs. Personally, I have set up an AI dedicated to writing novels on each of these platforms, which has allowed me to significantly optimize my writing process. I will soon provide you with all the information you need to access these tools.

# ChatGPT

ChatGPT artificial intelligence is a language model developed by OpenAI. It is an improved and more advanced version of its predecessor, GPT-3 (Generative Pre-trained Transformer 3). With ChatGPT-4, OpenAI sought to create AI that could hold natural conversations and provide consistent and relevant answers to questions asked by users.

ChatGPT is based on a neural network architecture called *GPT (Generative Pre-trained Transformer),* which has been revolutionary in the field of natural language processing. This architecture allows AI to understand and generate text contextually, taking into account the context of previous sentences to produce more accurate responses.

To train ChatGPT, OpenAI used a large dataset from the internet, which allowed it to learn how to recognize and reproduce complex linguistic structures. AI has been exposed to a wide variety of texts, ranging from news articles to books to online discussions. Through this training, ChatGPT has gained a deep knowledge of the language and is able to produce text fluently and consistently.

One of the key features of ChatGPT is its ability to generate text in a conversational way. AI can answer a wide variety of questions, provide detailed explanations, tell stories, and even simulate characters. It is designed to interact with users in a natural and intuitive way.

However, it's important to note that ChatGPT has its limitations. Sometimes, AI can produce answers that seem plausible, but are actually incorrect or inconsistent. It may also lack contextual understanding in certain situations and give answers that may seem disconnected from the question being asked. These limitations are mainly due to the biases and imperfections inherent in the training data and the model itself.

OpenAI is constantly working to improve ChatGPT and reduce these limitations. They also encourage users to provide feedback on errors and issues encountered in order to continue improving the AI.

By using ChatGPT, authors can benefit from its assistance in the writing process. AI can help generate ideas, provide word and sentence suggestions, help with proofreading and grammar correction, and even help develop characters and storylines. It can be a valuable tool to boost creativity and ease the flow of writing.

ChatGPT offers two types of access: the free subscription and the paid subscription. With free access, you can experiment and discover its features, opening up the possibility for a wide audience to interact with the AI and take advantage of its text-generating capabilities. However, the free plan has some limitations, such as restrictions on the number of requests that can be made over a period of time, as well as queues when there is high demand. In addition, the advanced features remain exclusive to paid subscribers.

When it comes to the ChatGPT AI paid subscription, OpenAI offers a subscription plan that offers additional benefits. With a paid subscription, you get priority access to AI, which means you can skip the lines and get answers faster. In addition, paid users get access to exclusive features and updates. This can include preview experimental features, enhanced language models, and additional customization options to meet your specific writing needs. The paid subscription is designed to provide a more comprehensive and flexible ChatGPT AI experience.

The paid subscription offers the possibility to use several bots1F[3] that you can use in the writing of your book. You can go to the laplumedigitale.com website for a list of the most commonly used bots and other additional information to this book.

In writing a novel, the free subscription may be sufficient, although limited. On the other hand, the paid subscription offers more possibilities, better writing quality and allows you to search for information online. The paid version also allows you to create high-quality images, making it easy to design your novel's cover. However, the paid subscription limits users to 40 queries per 3-hour block (at the time of writing this book), which limits the author's creative momentum.

About the free version (ChatGPT 3.5), it initially had an updated database until September 2021. However, recent information indicates that this deadline has been extended to January 2022. This means that, for the time being, you can benefit from access to more up-to-date data for your writing projects.

In short, while the free subscription can be used for writing a novel, the paid subscription offers additional benefits such as better writing quality, online search, high-quality image creation, and access to more up-to-date data. This can be especially beneficial for authors

---

[3] A ChatGPT bot is a computer program that uses artificial intelligence to simulate human conversations, capable of answering questions, offering information, and interacting with users in natural language.

who want to fully leverage the features of ChatGPT AI in the process of creating their novel.

To use ChatGPT, you need to go to the **https://chat.openai.com**. To register, click on "*Sign up*" (or "*Log In*" if you already have an account). To find all the video resources (including how to sign up for ChatGPT), I invite you to go to the **https://aidigitalpen.comwebsite.**

# POE

The poe.com is an online platform that offers a fast and useful conversational AI service. It provides the ability for users to engage with advanced artificial intelligence to get assistance in various areas. Poe stands out for its ability to provide quick and relevant answers, using advanced algorithms to understand and respond to user queries.

The website offers a range of chatbots that you can leverage for different tasks. What's special about POE is its ability to accommodate a variety of AI programming. I mentioned earlier that ChatGPT works with ChatGPT-3.5 or ChatGPT-4 programming. However, other equally powerful options are available, such as Claude, Mistral, Llama. Each of these programs has strengths and weaknesses, which is not to say that none is universally superior to the others. Therefore, you'll need to test different bots to determine which one best suits your writing style. Since these bots are created by a community of developers (of which I am a part), some of them come with a more rigorous build and offer better overall performance.

POE offers a free membership as well as a paid membership to get access to premium or higher quality bots.

## Examples of BOTS at POE

You'll discover a variety of bots suitable for a multitude of topics, each as diverse as the last. AI that specializes in cooking, traveling, learning, gaming, music, and more are at your disposal. In addition, a section entirely dedicated to writing is also available.

At the time of writing, most of the writing AIs available are in English, such as *LongBookWriter*, *FullBook-Writer*, *Novel-Writer*, *Scriptify*, and others. Although these programs are English-speaking, most can understand and produce texts in French. However, it's essential not to be fooled by attractive titles like "*LongBookWriter,*" which suggest writing a novel quickly. Due to AI limitations, the quality of the generated texts can be poor. It is therefore wise to use the strategies that I will present to you later in this book, to ensure the high quality of your writing.

You will find on the website of Ai BEYOND THE PEN, my suggestions for POE bots.

# Writing a novel with AI: How to use

# The Basics

Now that we've explored the basics of artificial intelligence, you've learned the skills to write instructions, and you see all the possibilities available to you, we're going to take the next step: writing a novel with AI. You could say that this crucial step comes late in this book, but it was important to explain in detail how to use AI and all its possibilities before you start writing. Without this information, your novel would have lacked quality and you wouldn't have been able to take full advantage of all that AI can bring to your writing.

There are different approaches to using artificial intelligence to compose your first novel. However, it is crucial to dispel a misconception that it is enough to ask AI to produce a 300-page science fiction novel in one go. In reality, depending on the type of artificial intelligence used, it will be able to generate a text with a maximum length ranging from 1000 to 1500 words, but by default, it will produce a text of about 500 words.

When using AI to write your novel, it's best to use it as a creative partner. You can start by giving her information about the genre, characters, or plot, and then work collaboratively with her to develop your story. You can ask them to generate ideas, descriptions, or dialogues, which you can then integrate and rework as you wish.

Using this approach, you can leverage the power of AI to boost your creativity and help you move forward in your writing process. Keep in mind that AI is a tool, and you always have control over the final content of your novel.

In addition, AI-written novels are usually simplistic at first and can quickly become boring. If you choose self-publishing and your book is available on Amazon, a boring novel is likely to get bad reviews from readers, resulting in limited sales of your book.

As an author, it's essential to bring your own voice, unique style, and creativity to your novel. This is what will allow you to create a captivating narrative and engage readers. Don't rely solely on an AI to write your book, but rather use it as an assistive tool to stimulate your imagination and improve your writing.

**Tips for Maximizing AI Efficiency**

In the world of AI-assisted writing, the key to maximizing efficiency lies in a thorough understanding of the tools available and a strategic approach to using them. First, it's essential to choose wisely the AI tool that best fits your specific writing needs. Some programs specialize in generating academic content, while others are designed to create fictional narratives. By selecting the most appropriate tool, you can maximize your chances of getting quality results.

Once you've chosen your tool, take the time to familiarize yourself with all of its features. Explore customization options, style settings, and control commands for text generation. The more comfortable you are with the tool, the more effectively you will be able to leverage it to meet your specific writing needs.

When giving instructions to the AI, be sure to be as specific as possible. Clearly define the parameters of your project, including the tone, style, and subject of the text you want to generate. The more specific your instructions are, the more relevant and quality the AI will be able to produce.

Once the AI has generated content, take the time to review it carefully. Identify passages that need adjustments or improvements and make any necessary changes. By refining the AI-generated results, you can improve the consistency and quality of the final text.

It's also important to remember to incorporate your own creativity into the writing process. AI can be a powerful tool for generating ideas and content, but it is not a substitute for human creativity. Use AI as a way to spark your imagination and generate suggestions, but don't let the algorithm dictate the end result entirely.

Finally, feel free to collaborate with other writers and experts to get the most out of AI in your writing process. Share your results with colleagues and solicit their feedback and suggestions. Their expertise can help you perfect your text and identify opportunities for improvement. It is also strongly advised to hire a professional reviewer, such as Alinea Solutions[4], to refine your work. Their expertise can make a significant improvement to your writing. By following these tips, you'll be able to maximize the effectiveness of AI in your writing process and produce top-quality copy, whether it's fiction, academic papers, or marketing content.

In the next few chapters, I'd like to share with you the method I personally use to create bestselling novels. By following this approach, you'll be able to produce a quality novel that will captivate readers.

---

[4] https://alinea.solutions

# The Limitations of ChatGPT

It's crucial to understand that even with all its power and intelligence, ChatGPT is not without its limitations.

One of the key limitations to consider is the length of text that ChatGPT can generate consistently. While it is capable of producing paragraphs or even entire pages of quality text, it may struggle to maintain that quality beyond 2000 words. Beyond that, they risk spreading themselves too thin, losing the thread of the story, or generating less relevant content.

This reality underscores the crucial importance of dividing your novel into manageable sections. By breaking down your work into chapters and then subdividing those chapters into smaller sections, you're providing ChatGPT with more digestible portions of text to process. This approach not only helps prevent the risk of loss of consistency, but it also provides a clear and organized structure to your story.

Personally, I've found that splitting each chapter into five separate sections works particularly well. This five-part division helps maintain balance in the flow of the story, while providing ChatGPT with clear milestones to develop the narrative smoothly and coherently.

By taking this approach, you maximize the chances of success of your collaboration with ChatGPT. You take advantage of its exceptional capabilities while mitigating the risks associated with its intrinsic limitations. In addition, this method allows you to maintain control over the progress of your novel, ensuring that each chapter moves harmoniously towards its conclusion.

In addition to dividing your novel into manageable sections, it's also essential to provide ChatGPT with additional guidance to guide its creation and maintain narrative consistency. After each AI-generated composition, it's a good idea to ask additional questions to clarify and deepen certain aspects of the story.

Here are some examples of additional questions you can ask ChatGPT:

*"Can you elaborate further on the main character of the story? What are their goals, motivations, and internal conflicts? »*

*"Could you describe in more detail the environment or setting in which this scene takes place? What are the elements that capture the characters' attention? »*

*"Could you introduce an element of suspense or tension into this part of the story? How can you keep the reader engaged until the next section? »*

*"What emotions are the characters feeling at this point in the story? How does this influence their actions and decisions? »*

Asking ChatGPT these additional questions help to refine and enrich the generated text, giving it a more precise direction and delving deeper into key aspects of the story. It also ensures that the AI remains focused and engaged in the progression of the narrative, avoiding narrative deviations or inconsistencies.

By incorporating this practice into your writing process, you'll fully exploit the collaborative potential offered by ChatGPT while maintaining creative control over your novel.

Incorporating dialogue into your novel adds an extra dimension to your narrative and makes the interactions between the characters livelier and more dynamic. Here's how you might give ChatGPT hints to add dialogs:

*"After the paragraph that talks about [insert specific topic or event], add dialogue between [character X's name] and [character Y's name]."*

By giving these precise cues to ChatGPT, you're guiding the AI to insert relevant and coherent dialogue in the right place in your narrative. This allows you to further personalize the generated content and make it more in line with your creative intentions.

Dialogue can be a powerful way to develop characters, advance the plot, and add emotional depth to your story. By asking ChatGPT to add dialogue at key moments in your novel, you can create more engaging and captivating scenes for your readers.

Note that ChatGPT will tend to answer the question simply. It's best to tell them after your question, *"Rewrite the paragraph with these adjustments,"* which will instruct them to not only respond to your request, but to rewrite the section WITH the requests you've made to them.

This clarification is essential to ensure that ChatGPT understands your intent and changes the text, accordingly, taking into account the additional instructions you have given it. By adding this clarification, you're guiding the AI to rewrite the section to include the requested adjustments, rather than just responding to the initial request.

Now that you understand the basics, let's get started.

# Let's write your first novel together

# Preparation

To start your novel with the help of AI, it's essential to define a few key elements that will guide the creation of prompts. Here are a few things to consider:

**Genre and theme**: Determine the genre of your novel (fantasy, sci-fi, romance, thriller, etc.) and the main themes you want to explore (love, quest for identity, fight against evil, etc.).

**Setting & Time**: Choose the setting (futuristic city, fantasy world, contemporary reality, etc.) and time (past, present, future) in which your story will take place.

**Main characters**: Think about the main characters in your story, their characteristics, their motivations, and how you envision them evolving.

**Main plot**: Outline the main plot of your novel. What is the central conflict? What are the obstacles that the characters will have to overcome?

# Some basics in writing a novel.

The aim of this book is to guide you in writing a novel using artificial intelligence. However, creating a bestselling book is much more complex. I don't want to give you an exhaustive training on how to write novels, but I do want to give you some basics.

## Develop Memorable Characters

At the heart of any literary masterpiece are rich and fascinating characters. Bringing complex, believable and endearing protagonists to life is the key to creating a captivating story that will leave a lasting impression. My exclusive method, based on the latest advances in artificial intelligence, will guide you in the careful elaboration of deep and authentic motivations. Feed your characters nuanced character traits and detailed personal stories to infuse them with a unique soul. Then, create a memorable romantic journey that will allow them to evolve, reinvent and transform themselves along the way.

Start by drawing the contours of a distinctive personality, paying particular attention to the psychology and moral values of your characters. Immerse yourself in their history, explore their relationships with those around them, examine the influences that shaped their temperament, and draw inspiration from historical, literary, or cinematic figures to inform your creations.

Give your characters their own goals and motivations, solidly rooted in their past and personality. These aspirations and impulses will guide their behavior, influence their actions, and shape the twists and turns of your plot. Focus on complex motivations, far from fixed archetypes and worn-out stereotypes, to give your characters a human and endearing dimension.

Finally, imagine a captivating story arc for each central character, articulating transitions and mutations. Encourage gradual evolution and profound transformation, encouraging your characters to question their certainties, face their fears and redefine their relationship to the world. A well-crafted narrative arc builds dramatic tension, providing the reader with moments of suspense, surprise, and satisfaction.

In short, cultivating memorable characters means establishing a delicate balance between individuality, motivation, and transformation. Take the time to fine-tune these key elements and watch your characters come to life, breathe and vibrate under your fingers, in the service of a breathless and addictive story.

**Build a cohesive world**

When you're building a world, whether it's grounded in reality or an entirely imaginary universe, it's crucial to make sure that the rules that govern that world are consistent and believable in the eyes of readers. This means that you need to clearly define the laws, boundaries, and consequences that govern your world, and stick to them throughout your narrative.

First, take some time to think about the foundations of your world. What are the political, economic and social systems in place? What are the beliefs, values, and traditions of the characters who live there? What supernatural powers, technologies, or beings exist in this universe? Once you've established these basics, you need to make sure that all of the characters' events, actions, and reactions are in line with these rules.

For example, if your world is ruled by an absolute monarchy, it would be inconsistent for a character to freely criticize the king without facing consequences. Similarly, if your universe is governed by strict magical laws, it is important that the users of magic abide by these rules or face logical consequences.

In addition, it is important to maintain some credibility in your world, especially if it is grounded in reality. Make sure events, technologies, and behaviors are realistic and plausible, given the times, geography, and culture of your world. For example, if your story is set in the Middle Ages, it would be unrealistic to describe cars or cell phones, unless it's euchronia or a specific sci-fi universe.

Finally, pay attention to the details and consistency of your world. Take notes on the different aspects of your universe and refer to them regularly to make sure you stay consistent. If a particular event or object is important in your story, describe it in detail for readers to refer to later. Also, don't be afraid to leave grey areas or mysteries in your world; This can encourage readers' imaginations and make them want to discover more.

**Create a captivating plot**

A captivating plot is a fundamental part of keeping the reader interested and engaged throughout your story. To achieve this, it is essential to introduce conflicts, twists and turns, and tense moments that keep readers turning the pages to find out what happens next.

First, focus on crafting a central conflict that will serve as the driving force behind your plot. This conflict can be internal (a character facing a moral dilemma or personal struggle) or external (a character facing an external antagonist, force, or situation). Whatever type of conflict you choose, make sure it's strong and engaging enough to entice readers to engage with your story.

Then, feel free to include unexpected twists and turns to surprise and captivate your readers. These elements of suspense and surprise can take a variety of forms, such as character revelations, unexpected plot twists, or unforeseen events that upset the characters' plans. By introducing these elements thoughtfully and strategically, you'll keep readers engaged and keep them reading.

Also, don't forget to include moments of tension and pressure to create a sense of urgency and danger. These moments can be generated by tight deadlines, looming threats, or insurmountable obstacles that put characters to the test. By creating intense and thrilling scenes, you'll keep readers' attention and get them emotionally invested in your story.

Finally, pay attention to the structure of your plot and the progression of the action. Make sure that the events are connected to each other and that the intensity of the story gradually increases, reaching a climax towards the end. Additionally, don't be afraid to slow down the pace from time to time to delve deeper into the characters, relationships, or themes in your story. By balancing moments of tension and intensity with calmer, reflective scenes, you'll provide readers with a rich and satisfying reading experience.

**Establish a rhythm**

Establishing a dynamic pace is key to keeping readers interested and engaged in your novel. To achieve this, alternate between moments of action and moments of calm, making sure that the story stays in motion and doesn't get bogged down in unnecessary lengths.

First, identify the key moments in your plot and determine which ones are worth developing in detail and which ones can be tackled more quickly. By balancing intense action scenes with quieter passages, you'll provide readers with a varied and engaging reading experience.

Then, alternate between moments of dialogue, description, and action to create a dynamic rhythm. Dialogue helps to advance the plot, reveal information about the characters, and create tensions or alliances. Descriptions are used to set the scene, describe the emotions and sensations of the characters, and create an immersive atmosphere. The action scenes, on the other hand, generate tension, suspense and intensity. By balancing these three types of scenes, you'll keep readers engaged and keep them reading.

Also, don't forget to include pauses and moments of reflection to allow readers to breathe and soak up the story. These moments can be in the form of bonding scenes, flashbacks or leaps into the future, evocative descriptions, or inner reflections of the characters. By providing readers with moments of calm and reflection, you'll allow them to become attached to the characters, understand what's at stake in the story, and immerse themselves in the world you've created.

Finally, pay attention to the progression of the action and the overall structure of your novel. Make sure that the events are connected to each other and that the intensity of the story gradually increases, reaching a climax towards the end. Also, don't be afraid to slow down the pace from time to time to provide readers with a rich and satisfying reading experience.

## Use the description sparingly

Descriptions are a crucial part of creating a vivid and immersive world in your novel. However, it's important not to overdo it and be careful not to slow down the pace of the story with descriptions that are too long or too detailed. To achieve this, use evocative and meaningful details that paint vivid mental images in the reader's mind, without weighing down the narrative.

First, identify the most important elements of your world and scenes, and focus on describing those details to create a rich and captivating universe. Choose details that reveal information about characters, times, places, or situations, and avoid getting lost in superfluous or plotless descriptions.

Then, use similes, metaphors, and figures of speech to brighten up your descriptions and make them more memorable. By using strong images and original comparisons, you will help readers imagine the scenes and immerse themselves in your world. Additionally, alternate between short, punchy descriptions and longer, detailed descriptions to create a dynamic and varied pace.

Also, pay attention to the order and progression of your descriptions. Start by outlining the most important or striking elements of your scenes, and leave the more subtle or secondary details for last. By structuring your descriptions in a thoughtful and strategic way, you'll help readers grasp the stakes of your scenes and immerse themselves in your world.

Finally, don't forget to use all five senses in your descriptions to provide a rich, sensorial reading experience. In addition to sight, which is often prioritized in descriptions, include details related to hearing, touch, smell, and taste to create an immersive and realistic atmosphere.

**Show, don't say**

Rather than just narrating the events to your readers, show them what's going on using the characters' actions, dialogue, and emotions. This approach will make your story more immersive, engaging, and memorable for readers.

First, focus on the details and nuances of your characters' actions, gestures, and expressions to show rather than say what's going on. By describing your characters' movements, postures, and reactions, you'll provide readers with a richer and more engaging reading experience.

Then, use dialogue to reveal the characters' thoughts, feelings, and motivations, rather than describing them directly. By staging authentic and meaningful conversations, you'll give readers a better understanding of the relationships between the characters, the stakes of the story, and the themes being addressed.

Also, don't forget to use the characters' emotions to show rather than describe what's going on. By describing the characters' emotional reactions to events, you will help readers identify with the characters, become attached to them, and feel empathy for them.

Also, pay attention to the order and progression of your scenes. Start by describing the most important or significant events and leave the more subtle or secondary details for last. By structuring your scenes thoughtfully and strategically, you'll help readers grasp the stakes of your scenes and immerse themselves in your world.

Dare to explore artificial intelligence to enhance your creative process. Don't miss out on the countless possibilities offered by these revolutionary tools. Whether you're a beginner or an experienced writer, challenge the limits of the imagination by opening yourself up to these cutting-edge technologies. Breathe new life into your stories by maximizing your productivity and boosting your inspiration. Our exclusive writing prompts, drawn from a library of hundreds of examples, will guide you step-by-step to create compelling stories. Trust our expertise and let AI transcend your art, without restricting your creativity.

## Describe the characters' surroundings

The description of places and buildings in a novel plays a crucial role in creating a believable and immersive literary world. It not only serves to situate the action in a geographical space, but it also contributes to the overall atmosphere of the work, enriches the psychology of the characters, and supports the evolution of the plot. This descriptive dimension is a delicate art, where the balance between too much and too little can significantly influence the reader's experience.

First, describing a place or a building well anchors the story in a tangible reality, offering the reader a precise spatio-temporal framework. This geographical immersion facilitates the reader's identification and empathy with the characters, allowing them to visualize the scenes as if they were there. The importance is in the details: a cobblestone street lit by old-fashioned street lamps may evoke a bygone era, while a glass and steel skyscraper emphasizes modernity and perhaps isolation in contemporary megacities.

Secondly, the descriptions of the environments influence the atmosphere of the novel. A dilapidated house, with its broken windows and overgrown garden, can create an atmosphere of mystery or melancholy, preparing the reader for dark revelations or tragic events. Conversely, a sunny square lined with lively cafes can create a cheerful and lighthearted atmosphere. The places then become full-fledged actors in the story, whose architectural and atmospheric characteristics resonate with the themes addressed and the tone adopted.

In addition, the description of the places enriches the characterization of the characters. A protagonist who feels at home in the vibrant chaos of a popular market reveals a different nature from a character who prefers the solitude of dusty libraries. The characters' interactions with their environment, the way they perceive and describe places, offer valuable insights into their personalities, tastes, and even their past.

Places also have an essential narrative function. They can be the scene of key events in the novel, intersections of destinies, or spaces of revelation. A bridge can symbolize a transition or a choice, a labyrinth, an inner quest; a boundary, the moral boundaries that the characters are willing to cross. The way locations are integrated into the narrative contributes to the dynamics of the plot, enriching the text with subtext and symbols.

Finally, a careful description of the places and buildings invites a more sensory and emotional reading. By describing textures, colors, sounds, and smells, the author stimulates the reader's imagination, immersing them in a deeper and richer literary experience. This multisensory approach enhances immersion and allows the reader to experience the novel in a more intense way.

In short, the description of places and buildings is much more than just a backdrop for the action, it is a vital component of the narrative that enriches the world of the novel, roots the story in a believable space, ignites the reader's imagination, and gives emotional and symbolic resonance to the entire work. An author who has mastered the art of spatial description thus offers a gateway to fictional worlds where each reader is invited to lose themselves and be amazed.

**Review & Edit**

Editing is an essential and unavoidable step in the writing process, whether it's a story written by a human being or generated by artificial intelligence. Take the time to carefully proofread, review, and edit your work to eliminate mistakes, refine style, and strengthen the story.

First, pay attention to grammar, spelling, and punctuation to ensure that your text is free of mistakes and easy to read. Use online remediation tools or dedicated apps to detect common errors and fix them quickly. Additionally, don't forget to check the coherence and logic of your story, especially if you're using an AI to build your narrative.

Next, focus on improving the style and tone of your text. Look for repetitions, sentences that are too long or too complex, and awkward or awkward turns of phrase. Replace them with simpler, clearer, and more impactful wording, making sure to preserve the voice and tone of your story.

Also, pay attention to the structure and progression of your story. Make sure that the events are connected to each other, and that the intensity of the story gradually increases, reaching a climax towards the end. Also, make sure that the transitions between scenes are smooth and logical, and that the issues and themes of your story are clear and consistent.

Also, don't forget to assess the emotional impact and engagement of your story. Ask yourself if your characters are developed and engaging enough, if the conflicts and stakes are strong and engaging enough, and if the themes and messages in your story are deep and meaningful enough.

Finally, pay attention to the voice and tone of your story. Make sure your style, language, and tone are consistent and relevant to your target audience, and that your story reflects your vision and message.

By following these basics, you'll be better equipped to write a captivating and memorable novel.

With that in mind, here are some prompts you could use to start your novel:

> **Prompt 1: Introduction to the World**
>
> *"Imagine a world where* **[describe setting and time]**, *populated by* **[types of characters, creatures, societies]**. *In this world,* **[introduce a unique element or specific technology]** *has changed the way people live. Describe this world in detail, emphasizing* **[a specific aspect related to your theme]**. *»*

Imagine a world where in the year 2025, populated by robots controlled by artificial intelligence. In this world, AI has changed the way people live. Describe this world in detail, with a focus on how humans manage to live with AIs.

*In the year 2025, in this world where robots are ubiquitous and controlled by advanced artificial intelligence, the daily lives of human beings have been transformed in profound and often surprising ways.*

*First of all, AI has revolutionized the world of work. Repetitive and monotonous tasks are now performed by robots, freeing up humans to focus on more creative, intellectual, and social pursuits. Industries such as manufacturing, logistics, agriculture, and even healthcare have been largely automated, increasing efficiency and reducing human error...*

Introduce Liam, a computer technician who lives in a barn. It is unique because it can change the code of AIs. Now, the AIs decide to exterminate humans, marking the beginning of his quest to annihilate AI robots. Describe their first reaction and the first step they take.

*Liam sat in his barn, surrounded by flashing computer monitors and intertwined cables. As a self-taught computer technician, he had always been fascinated by the inner workings of AIs and possessed a rare skill: the ability to modify their code.*

*When the first reports of AI bot attacks on humans began to filter through the media, Liam felt an icy chill run down his spine. His only advantage over these machines, his ability to hack their code, was now of crucial importance to the survival of humanity...*

**Prompt 3: Initial Conflict**

"**[Main character's name]** *encounters its first major obstacle:* [**describe the conflict**]. *This conflict is related to* [**theme or issue of the novel**]. *Explain how he/she is trying to overcome this obstacle and the immediate consequences of his/her actions.* »

Liam encounters his first big obstacle: The AIs discover Liam's existence and purpose. This conflict is related to saving humans from extermination. Explain how they are trying to overcome this obstacle and the immediate consequences of their actions.

*When the AIs discovered Liam's existence and purpose, an inevitable conflict erupted. Aware of his ability to manipulate their code and thwart their plans, the AI bots saw him as a major threat to their existence.*

**Prompt 4: Character Interaction**

"*Create a scene where* [**name of main character**] *meet* [**name of another important person**] *in* [**location**]. *Their meeting is crucial because* [**reason**]. *They discuss* [**topic**], *which reveals* [**an important aspect of their character or plot**]. »

Create a scene where Liam meets Amelia, in a resistance clan. Meeting them is crucial, as she is also a computer coder. They discuss hacking AIs, which reveals how difficult it is to get into the mainframe.

*In the darkness of the Resistance Clan's makeshift meeting room, Liam stood in front of a whiteboard covered in complex network diagrams and lines of code. As he tried to solve a major security issue, the door slowly opened, revealing a female figure.*

*"I see you're deep in thought," said a soft, but determined voice. It was Amelia, a renowned computer coder within the resistance clan.*

*Liam looked up to meet her gaze. "Amelia, it's a surprise to see you here. What brings you here? »*

*"I've heard you're having trouble with AI security," she replied as she approached. "I thought maybe I could help you."*

---

**Prompt 5: Turning Point**

*"At a crucial point in the story,* **[main character's name]** *has to make a difficult choice that will have consequences for everything else in the story. The choice is between* **[option A]** *and* **[option B],** *each of which has implications* **[description of implications].** *Describe his inner struggle and the final choice. »*

At a crucial moment in the story, Liam must make a difficult choice that will have consequences for everything else in the story. The choice is between rallying behind the AIs or fighting with Amelia, each with implications for the fate of humanity. Describe his inner struggle and the final choice.

*As tension mounted and the battle between human forces and AIs reached its climax, Liam found himself torn between two paths, each offering unique promises and perils.*

*On the one hand, rallying behind the AIs seemed to offer a more immediate and perhaps less bloody way out of the struggle. The machines promised security and stability, claiming that in exchange for his cooperation, Liam and those following him could be spared from impending destruction. This path had the lure of survival, but at the cost of compromising the values and ideals for which he had fought so hard.*

# Setting up chapters

Choosing the right chapters for your novel involves structuring your narrative in such a way that each chapter serves to advance the story, develop your characters, and keep the reader engaged. Here's an example of a prompt to help you design the chapters of your novel, assuming you already have a basic idea of your plot and characters:

Start by asking me how many chapters I want to have for my novel. Depending on the number of chapters, you'll have to structure the novel as follows: the first chapter offers an introduction to the story and the main character, the first chapter, which counts for 10% of the novel, talks about the initial situation by introducing the secondary characters, then 20% of the next chapters will be about the disturbing element, the next 40% will be the twists and turns,  The next 20% will be the resolution elements and the last 10% will be the final situation and conclusion of the novel.

*Perfect, with 15 chapters, here's how I would structure your novel:*

*Introduction (Chapter 1): 10% of the novel*

*Introduction to the story and the main character.*

*Setting up the framework and key issues.*

*Introducing the supporting characters.*

*Initial situation (Chapters 2 to 4): 30% of the novel (10% per chapter)*

*Development of the initial situation.*

*Deepening of the relationships between the characters.*

*Introduction of key plot elements.*

*Disruptive Element (Chapters 5 & 6): 20% of the novel (10% per chapter)*

*Introduction of the main disruptive element.*

*Characters' initial reactions to this disruption.*

*Increased tension and suspense.*

*Adventures (Chapters 7 to 11): 40% of the novel (8% per chapter)*

*Development of the major events of the plot.*

*Confrontations, twists and revelations.*

*Rise of action and conflict.*

*Resolution Elements (Chapters 12 and 13): 20% of the novel (10% per chapter)*

*Development of possible solutions to conflicts and challenges.*

*Planning and implementation of the resolution.*

*Progress to the conclusion.*

*Final situation and conclusion (Chapters 14 and 15): 20% of the novel (10% per chapter)*

*Final resolution of the main conflicts and the story arcs of the characters.*

*An epilogue or conclusion that leaves a lasting impression on the reader.*

*This structure will help maintain a good narrative rhythm while developing the plot and characters in a balanced way. Of course, you can adjust this structure according to the specific needs of your story!*

Once the structure of the novel is in place, you can ask the AI to detail each chapter:

From this structure, give me the title of each chapter with a short description for each of them.

*Of course! Here are the titles and descriptions for each chapter based on the previous structure:*

### The Beginning

*Introduction to the story and introduction to the main character, Liam.*

*Setting up the framework and the stakes of the story.*

*Introducing the supporting characters and their relationship with Liam.*

### The Roots of the Conflict

*Development of the initial situation.*

*Exploration of the characters' motivations and goals.*

*Setting up the key plot elements.*

*( ... )*

Don't hesitate to ask the AI for any changes you find necessary, such as: *"I don't like the title of chapter 5, suggest something else"* or *"I don't like the topics in chapter 12, suggest something else"*. This way, you will have the desired structure for your novel.

## Writing Chapters

As mentioned, AI will have a hard time writing an entire novel. The same is true if he is asked to write an entire chapter. The chapter will usually be too short.

The average length of a chapter in a novel can vary greatly depending on the author's writing style, literary genre, and editorial preferences. However, to give you a general estimate, a typical chapter in a novel can contain between 2000 and 5000 words.

Of course, there are exceptions to this range. Some chapters can be shorter, with only a few hundred words, while others can be much longer, easily exceeding 5000 words. The length often depends on the nature of the plot, the events unfolding in the chapter, and how the author chooses to structure their story.

Ultimately, the main goal is to keep the reader engaged and move the plot forward in an efficient manner, no matter how long each chapter is.

 Here is an example of a prompt request to illustrate this situation (please note that I will not write the full text transmitted by the AI in order to facilitate the reading of the examples):

*Chapter 1: The Beginning*

*Part 1: The Dawn of a New Era*

*Liam stood on the threshold of his barn, watching the rising sun bathe the surrounding countryside in golden light. The morning wind gently stirred the leaves of the trees, while the first birdsong announced the beginning of a new day. For many, this idyllic scene would evoke peace and tranquility, but for Liam, it represented the calm before the impending storm.*

*Ever since he was a child, Liam had always been drawn to the mysteries of technology and computing. While his classmates were passionate about games and sports, Liam preferred to spend his hours dismantling and repairing computers in the attic of the family home. His inquisitive mind and passion for problem-solving had led him to become a self-taught computer expert.*

*(....)*

*Number of words in the first part: 280 words*

Even if you ask the AI to write a block with a minimum of 1000 words, it is common for the text produced to be usually shorter, depending on the type of AI used. In such cases, it is necessary to ask for additional details on certain paragraphs to ensure that the content is complete and satisfactory.

*Chapter 1: The Beginning*

*Part 1: The Dawn of a New Era*

*Liam stood on the threshold of his barn, watching with some solemnity the majestic spectacle of the rising sun bathing the surrounding countryside in golden light. The first rays of morning embraced the green fields, chasing away the darkness of the night and heralding the advent of a new day. The cool breeze of dawn gently caressed her face, bringing with it the unmistakable smell of damp earth and blooming flowers.*

*For many, this idyllic scene would evoke peace and tranquility, but for Liam, it meant so much more than that. It was the calm before the impending storm, the moment when the world seemed suspended in anticipation of a cataclysmic event. A palpable tension hung in the air, sending shivers down Liam's spine despite the rising heat of the rising sun.*

*(...) Word count in the first part: 379 words*

As you note, AI has a hard time getting a minimum of 500 words. It should be taken into consideration that this text was generated with ChatGPT version 3.5 (the free version). The paid version (4.0) allows you to write more words (without ever getting to 1000 words. However, at the time of writing this book, version 4 allows a maximum of 40 prompts to be placed in a 3-hour period. Which can break a writing spurt.

We will therefore request additional information on this initial section in order to increase the volume of text. It is necessary to ask him to elaborate on certain paragraphs:

In the first paragraph, you say that he "is on the threshold of a barn." You also speak of a "surrounding countryside of golden light". Rewrite this first paragraph, giving more details about the barn and the countryside. Then specifies the number of words in the old paragraph and the number of words in the new paragraph.

*Liam stood on the threshold of his old wooden barn, his hands resting lightly on the rustic railing that had seen decades of sun and rain pass by. Behind him, the scaled, grizzled planks of the structure bore witness to its venerable age, while the corrugated iron roof reflected the first rays of the rising sun ( ... ) dressed in a mosaic of shimmering greens and golden yellows, while the century-old trees stood like silent guardians, their leaves quivering gently in the morning breeze.*

*The old paragraph had 42 words, while the new paragraph contained 68 words.*

The most observant will have noted that even though the AI indicates that the first paragraph is (according to him) 42 words, it actually has 71 words. So, you will then have a longer text than expected, which will be perfect for having a story with the minimum word count for your novel. To get an exact idea of the number of words for each text or paragraph, I invite you to go to the Word Counter website ( **https://wordcounter.net** ) which will tell you the number of words for each part for free.

I understand that this method is more time-consuming than just asking the AI to write a book. However, not only is it more entertaining in the creation of your novel, but it also allows for further customization of your story. Plus, it makes your novel much more captivating to read, which will guarantee you better reviews on platforms like Amazon. As a result, you'll be more successful as an author, with more sales and recognition.

# Harnessing AI for Effective Storytelling

# Narrative structure

In this chapter, we'll discuss a crucial but often overlooked aspect of creative writing: building an effective narrative structure. A solid architecture is essential to guide your readers through a captivating and memorable journey, providing them with a cohesive and satisfying narrative experience. Fortunately, artificial intelligence can prove to be a valuable ally in this endeavour, assisting you in the organization and structuring of your story. Together, we'll look at the different types of narrative structures, how they can be applied, and how AI can help you implement them to bring your story to life.

## Introduction to Narrative Structures

Narrative structure is the pillar that supports a novel, giving it a form and flow that takes the reader through the story. It's a road map for the author, defining the path the story will take from beginning to end.

Typically, a narrative structure is composed of several key elements: the exposition, which sets the scene and introduces the characters; The trigger, which initiates the main action. development, where tensions and challenges are built; the climax, the climax of the action; and finally, the resolution, where the plot finds its conclusion.

Each story varies in its structure, and the use of AI can help customize that structure to best serve the narrative the author wants to tell. AI can suggest variations of these basic elements to create a story that is not only structured, but also resonates with originality and creativity.

Using AI in developing a narrative structure can also help identify recurring motifs and themes in the author's genre, offering patterns that have proven to work with readers. With an in-depth analysis of large literary corpora, AI can guide the author towards narrative structures that have proven to be captivating and satisfying.

In terms of challenges, the protagonists of a story may face a variety of obstacles, whether internal, such as fighting their own fears or desires, or external, such as adversaries or hostile environments. AI can help modulate these challenges to ensure that they effectively contribute to character growth and plot progression.

Additionally, a solid narrative structure helps maintain an adequate pace, balancing fast-paced action scenes with quieter moments of reflection, ensuring that the reader stays engaged from start to finish. AI, with its ability to analyze data, can help adjust the pace to maximize the emotional impact of the story.

The integration of AI into the structuring of a novel thus allows unprecedented flexibility and precision in the art of storytelling. It offers authors the means to move beyond traditional formulas and explore new narrative dimensions, enriching their narrative with layers of complexity and depth that were previously out of reach.

# Types of narrative structures and their applications

Narrative structures are essential in the construction of a novel, as they guide how the story unfolds and keeps the reader engaged. Here are some of the most common narrative structures used in literature.

## The Linear Structure

Linear structure, also known as chronological structure, is one of the most prevalent and simple-to-understand types of narrative. In a linear structure, the events of history unfold in the order in which they occur, following the logical sequence of time. It usually starts with an introduction to the world and characters, followed by the development of events, leading to a climax, and concludes with a resolution.

Let's take the example of a classic adventure novel: a young hero leaves his home to embark on a journey. He overcomes various obstacles, meets new allies, faces the main antagonist, and after a decisive confrontation, he returns home, changed and wiser. A famous example of this type of structure is J.R.R. Tolkien's "The Hobbit," where Bilbo Baggins leaves the Shire, goes through a series of adventures in sequential order, and returns home, transformed by his experiences.

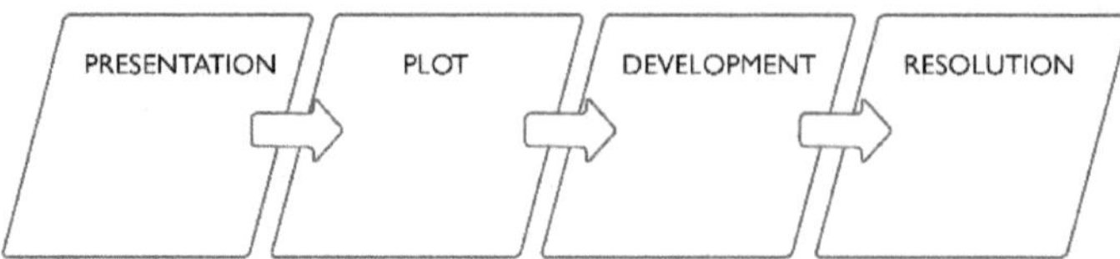



## The three-act structure

The three-act structure is a classic narrative model that divides a story into three distinct parts: introduction or set-up, development or confrontation, and resolution. This framework provides a clear blueprint for developing the narrative, allowing the audience to easily follow the evolution of the story. An emblematic example of this structure is Francis Ford Coppola's film "The Godfather", where the first act introduces the Corleone family and the world of the mafia, the second act shows the rise of conflicts and challenges, and the third act concludes with Michael Corleone's consolidation of power and conflict resolution.

The three-act structure

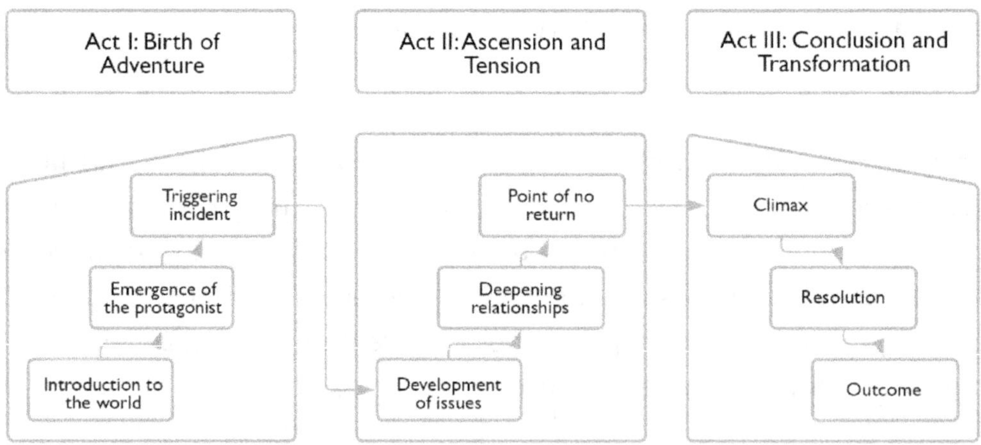

## The eight-point structure

The eight-point structure, designed to enrich narrative development, includes the initial stage, the trigger, the first turn, the middle, the second turn, the point of no return, the climax, and the conclusion. An illustrative example is "Harry Potter and the Sorcerer's Stone": Harry discovers that he is a wizard, joins Hogwarts (trigger), faces various challenges and mysteries (twists), discovers that the Philosopher's Stone is threatened, and finally, prevents Voldemort from obtaining it (climax), concluding his year with new friendships and lessons learned.

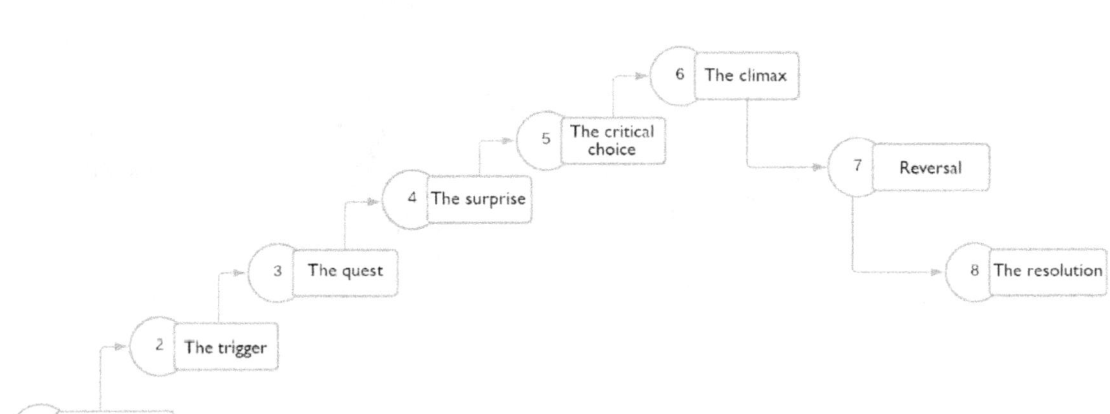


## The Hero's Journey

The structure of the hero's journey, developed by Joseph Campbell, describes the typical path the protagonist takes in an adventure. It includes the call to adventure, the rejection of the call, the supernatural help, the crossing of the first threshold, the trials, the approach, the supreme test, the reward, the way back, the resurrection, and the return with the elixir. A classic example is "Star Wars: A New Hope," where Luke Skywalker follows this journey, from his call to adventure by Obi-Wan Kenobi to his transformation into a hero and triumphant return.

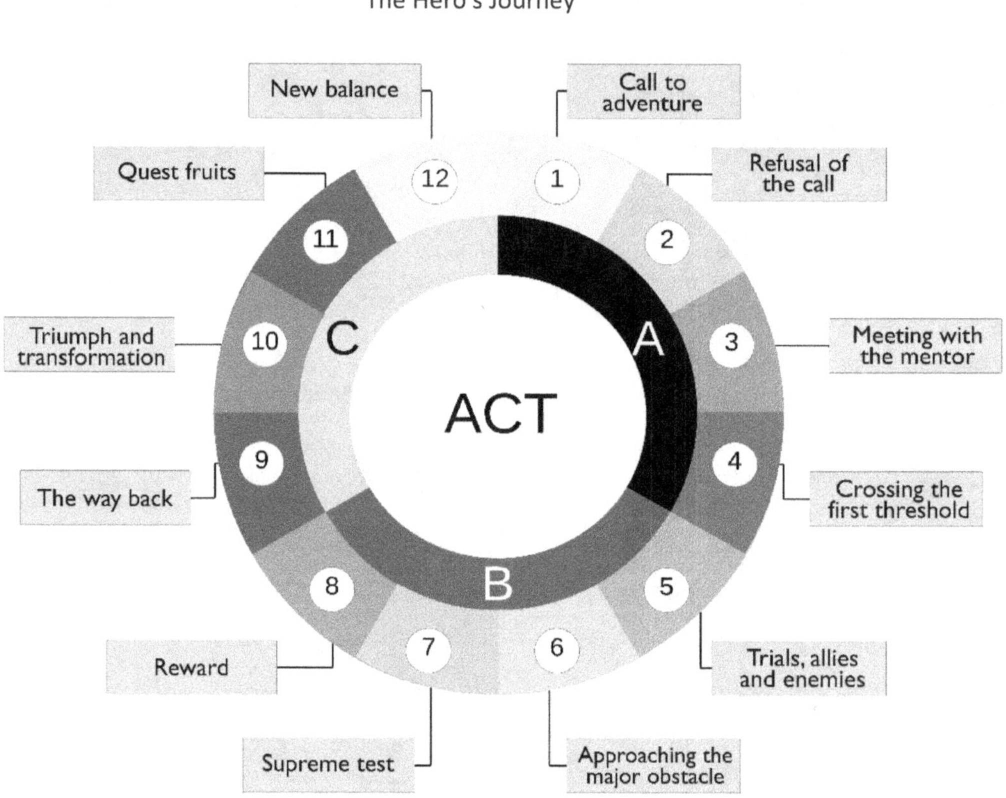



## The Fichtean Curve

Fichtean's Curved Structure, named after playwright John Gardner, is characterized by a series of rises and falls in the action to keep the reader engaged. It begins with exposition, followed by escalating crises that culminate in a climax, before resolving the plot. A prominent example is Daphne du Maurier's "Rebecca," where the story escalates through revelations and conflicts around the mystery of Rebecca, culminating in the truth about her death, before concluding with the resolution of tensions between the characters.

The Fichtean Curve

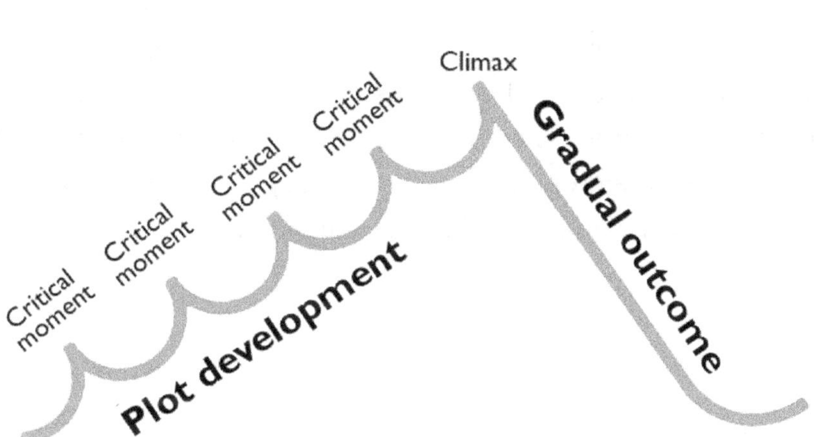


## The structure of the "Story Circle"

The structure of Dan Harmon's "Story Circle" is an approach to storytelling that breaks down the story into eight essential steps. Dan Harmon, creator of the TV series "Community" and co-creator of "Rick and Morty," was inspired by Joseph Campbell's Hero's Journey structure to develop his model. The "Story Circle" is designed to be flexible and applicable to different types of stories, providing a framework that helps writers structure their narratives in a cohesive and engaging way. This structure by Dan Harmon is prized for its simplicity and versatility, allowing writers to create deep and meaningful narratives while maintaining a strong narrative structure.

"The Walking Dead" series deploys the narrative structure of Dan Harmon's Story Circle to orchestrate the evolution and challenges of its characters in a post-apocalyptic world.

From the beginning, we see Rick Grimes, the protagonist, in his comfort zone as the sheriff before the world collapses under the zombie apocalypse. His desire to reunite with his family pushes him out of this zone, introducing him to an unknown and terrifying world. Throughout the series, Rick and his group adapt to this hostile new environment, learning to survive in the face of constant threats from both the undead and the living.

Each season reflects the stages of the "Story Circle," with moments of achievement and sacrifice that test the characters and make them evolve. For example, the loss of loved ones and the need to make morally ambiguous choices embody the cost of their survival. Despite these hardships, the group always finds a way to return to some semblance of normalcy, seeking a new refuge or forming new alliances.

## The circular structure

The Circular Structure Is a narrative design where the story ends at the point where it began, thus forming a circle. This may reflect a cyclical development of the character or thematize the idea of fate. A classic example is "The Alchemist" by Paulo Coelho, where the protagonist, Santiago, goes in search of treasure, travels through landscapes and spiritual experiences, only to discover that the real treasure was buried in his home, where his journey began.

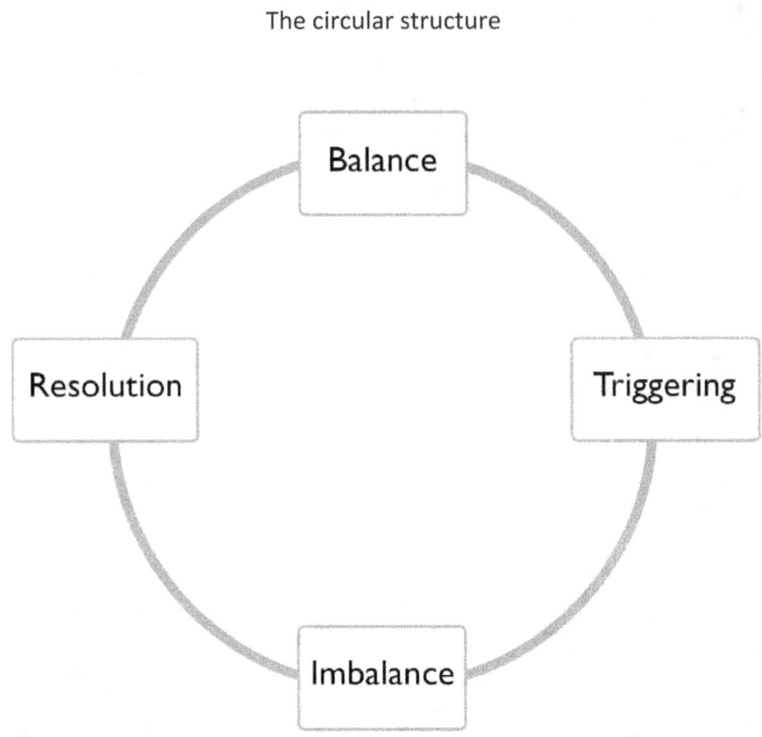



## Non-linear structure

The non-linear structure in the narrative breaks with the traditional chronological sequence, blending events from different moments in ways that are not immediately sequential. This creates a more dynamic and engaging reading experience, inviting readers to put the pieces of the puzzle together on their own. A famous example is Quentin Tarantino's "Pulp Fiction," which, despite being a movie, exemplifies this technique perfectly with its intertwined stories presented in a non-chronological order, enriching the overall narrative through this structured choice.

# How AI Can Help You Organize and Structure Your Novel

Artificial intelligence (AI) is a valuable ally for authors in structuring their novel. With its data analysis and processing capabilities, AI can offer suggestions and tools to strengthen narrative structure and ensure consistency throughout the story.

It helps authors define the basic structure of their novel by analyzing the conventions of different literary genres. By studying a large body of existing work, the AI can identify the most common and effective narrative structures for each genre, such as the three-act structure for an adventure novel or the five-act structure for a tragedy.

Once the basic structure is set, AI can help plan key plot points, such as exposition, turning points, climax, and resolution. By analyzing best practices from bestselling novels, she can suggest the perfect time to introduce these important elements and ensure a captivating narrative pacing.

Successful novels often feature multiple intertwined narrative arcs, each with its own beginning, middle, and end. AI can help authors develop and organize these story arcs by identifying the key elements of each arc and ensuring that they are properly integrated into the overall structure of the novel.

Characters are at the heart of any novel, and their development must be carefully integrated into the narrative structure. AI can help writers manage their characters' transformation arcs by suggesting key moments for their evolution and ensuring that their development is consistent with the main plot.

One of the major challenges in writing a novel is maintaining perfect consistency and continuity throughout the story. The AI can analyze the entire text and spot potential inconsistencies in plot details, character characteristics, or elements of the fictional universe. It can then suggest adjustments to address these issues and ensure a smooth reading experience.

A well-balanced novel should have a harmonious blend of action, character development, description, and dialogue. AI can help authors balance these different elements by analyzing their distribution in the text and proposing adjustments if necessary, to avoid lengths or sections that are too dense.

After completing an initial draft, authors can receive valuable feedback from their editors, critics, or beta readers. AI can help them analyze this feedback and identify sections of the structure that need tweaking, whether it's to clarify certain points, deepen character development, or strengthen overall consistency.

By leveraging AI's analytics and data processing capabilities, authors can receive valuable support to structure their novel in a robust and coherent way.

# Examples of prompts to structure your story

When embarking on writing a novel with the help of artificial intelligence, it is crucial to define the desired narrative structure from the start. By providing the AI with a clear and detailed prompt on the chosen structure, we ensure that it will be able to generate consistent and style-friendly content throughout the creation process. Here are a few reasons why this initial step is essential.

## Maintain narrative coherence

A successful novel should have a strong narrative coherence, with a clear thread that guides the reader from exposition to final resolution. Specifying the narrative structure early on allows the AI to understand the expectations and conventions of the chosen genre, style, or form. Whether it's the classic three-act structure, non-linear storytelling, or any other innovative approach, AI will be able to generate content that fits perfectly into this structural logic.

## Respecting gender conventions

Each literary genre has its own conventions in terms of narrative structure. A thriller usually requires a build-up of tension to a gripping climax, while a romantic comedy often follows a more predictable structure. By indicating the genre and associated expectations in the initial prompt, the AI can adapt accordingly and produce content that respects the codes and expectations of readers of that genre.

## Facilitate planning and organization

Defining the narrative structure early on helps make it easier to plan and organize the novel. This allows the AI to suggest key development points, moments to introduce twists and turns, or secondary narrative arcs, while respecting the overall structure. This can go a long way in helping authors stay focused and avoid digressions or inconsistencies.

## Ensuring a balanced narrative rhythm

A good narrative pacing is essential to captivate readers. By clarifying the structure, the AI can identify the right moments to insert action scenes, moments of descriptive pause, or character development, in order to maintain a balanced and engaging pace throughout the narrative.

## Develop cohesive personas

Characters are at the heart of any novel, and their development must be carefully integrated into the narrative structure. By providing information about the structure from the get-go, the AI can suggest appropriate times to evolve characters, introduce their transformation arcs, and ensure that their development is consistent with the main plot.

**Allow for adjustments along the way**

Even with a well-defined initial structure, it is sometimes necessary to make adjustments during the writing process. By having access to the basic structure, the AI can propose minor changes or reorganizations while preserving the overall coherence of the narrative.

By creating a clear and detailed prompt on the chosen narrative structure from the beginning of the writing process with AI, authors offer themselves a major asset to ensure consistency, respect for genre conventions, a balanced pacing and harmonious character development. This allows them to focus on the creative aspects of writing, while knowing that the AI will make sure to keep the style and structure established.

**Example of prompts**

Here are some examples of start prompts for different styles of narrative structure:

**Classical three-act structure**

<u>Generic Novel:</u>

*"For this novel, I'd like to follow a classic three-act structure. In the first act, introduce the world, the main characters, and their goals. Also, introduce a disturbing element that will kick off the plot. The second act should explore the obstacles and complications faced by the characters as they try to achieve their goals. Gradually build up the tension to the climax. The third act should present the final confrontation, the resolution of the main conflict, and the conclusion of the story. »*

Thriller:

*"I want to write a fast-paced thriller with a three-act structure. In the first act, introduce the protagonist, a private investigator, or an ordinary person, and the trigger that will put them in a dangerous situation (a murder mystery, a conspiracy, etc.). The second act is expected to explore the obstacles faced by the protagonist as he investigates and gets closer to the truth, with twists and turns and red herrings to keep the tension going. In the third act, solve the main plot and its ramifications. »*

Romantic Comedy:

*"For this three-act romantic comedy, start by presenting the two main characters in opposite situations of their love/relationship lives. The disturbing element of the first act should bring them together in unexpected ways. The second act will explore the comic obstacles to their budding relationship, such as misunderstandings, personality differences, or embarrassing circumstances. Build up the tension in love until the climax where they will have to overcome a major challenge. In the third act, they should finally resolve their differences and reunite. »*

Adventure Novel:

*"I'd like a classic three-act structure for an epic adventure/fantasy novel. In the first act, establish the imaginary world, introduce the hero as well as the threat/quest that will start the plot. The second act is expected to see the hero assemble a team, face off against challenges and fantastical creatures, while uncovering secrets about the main antagonist/threat. Culminate this second act with a big battle or revelation. In the third act, the hero will face the antagonist in a decisive final confrontation to save his world. »*

<u>Family Drama:</u>

*"For this three-act family drama, start by presenting the tense/problematic family dynamics in the first act, with a particular event that will exacerbate existing tensions. The second act will explore interpersonal conflicts, unspoken words and old wounds resurfacing, with tension rising to a breaking point. In the third act, the characters will have to face painful, but liberating truths, in the hope of reconciling or at least finding some peace/acceptance. »*

**8-point structure**

<u>Structure of the Learning Story:</u>

*"I want to write a learning/training novel with an 8-point structure:*

1. *Introduce the protagonist in his or her initial environment*
2. *The triggering event that challenges one's way of life*
3. *The protagonist leaves his familiar surroundings*
4. *Early Experiences in the New World*
5. *A mentor or a key meeting that advances their development*
6. *A major test or challenge that tests their new skills*
7. *A revelation or a profound realization*
8. *The protagonist returns transformed to his home world. »*

Detective novel:

"For this detective novel, structure the plot in 8 key points:

1. The Initial Crime Scene
2. The Investigator's Initial Investigations
3. False leads appear
4. A new discovery relaunches the investigation
5. The main suspect has been identified
6. An unexpected twist
7. The Final Confrontation with the Culprit
8. The resolution of the case and its consequences

Build a suspenseful and twisted plot around these important milestones in the police investigation. »


Historical novel:

"I'd like an 8-point structure for an epic historical novel:

1. The historical context is established
2. The main protagonists are introduced
3. A conflict or major event breaks out
4. The protagonists are plunged into turmoil
5. New Alliances and Strategies Are Forming
6. A great battle or confrontation takes place
7. The consequences of this battle are reverberating
8. A new era/order settles in at the end of the conflict

Develop a complex yet realistic storyline based on historical events and figures while infusing drama and epic. »

Romantic Comedy:

*"For this romantic comedy, let's use an 8-act structure:*

1. *Introduce the two main characters*
2. *The Initial Tense Encounter/A Misunderstanding*
3. *A first pull is formed in spite of them*
4. *External obstacles stand in the way of their relationship*
5. *A comedic climax where all seems lost*
6. *Awareness of their true feelings*
7. *The act of bravery/grand gesture to reconcile*
8. *Their final union and the future that lies ahead of them*

*Develop a plot that is both light and moving, balancing comedic elements and moments of sincerity between the two characters. »*

Horror Novel:

*"For this horror novel, let's follow a terrifying 8-point structure:*

1. *An ordinary/reassuring setting*
2. *The Disruptive Element/First Manifestation*
3. *A deceptive lull, the horror becomes clearer*
4. *Things are getting worse, the threat is rising*
5. *A First Confrontation/Sacrifice*
6. *Survivors are hunted down, the most intense moments*
7. *The Inevitable Confrontation with Horror*
8. *Final resolution, but at what cost?*

*Build an eerie atmosphere and moments of outright terror around this structure by advancing the threat in an oppressive way. »*

**Hero's Journey Structure**

<u>Epic & Fantasy:</u>

*"I want to write an epic fantasy novel following the classic structure of the 12-Step Hero's Journey:*

1. *The Ordinary World*
2. *The Call to Adventure*
3. *Denial of the appeal*
4. *Meeting with the mentor*
5. *Crossing the first threshold*
6. *Trials, Allies, Enemies*
7. *The Approach to the Deepest Cave*
8. *The Ultimate Test*
9. *The Reward*
10. *The Way Back*
11. *The Resurrection*
12. *The return with the elixir*

*Develop a thrilling heroic quest through a rich and immersive fantasy world, building the full hero transformation arc according to these 12 initiatory stages. »*

<u>Chronicles of Modern Life:</u>

*"For these chronicles of modern life, let's use the flexible structure of The Hero's Journey:*

1. *The Ordinary World (The Initial Routine)*
2. *The Call to Adventure (an event that shakes up the routine)*
3. *Temporary refusal of change*
4. *Meeting with a mentor/awareness*
5. *Taking the first step towards change*
6. *Early Experiences/Progress and Challenges*
7. *The Approach of a Major Turning Point*
8. *The Litmus Test (Crucial Choice)*

9. Inner Reward (New Perspective)
10. Integration of changes
11. A symbolic rebirth/resurrection
12. Mastering the new way of life

*Explore the arcs of learning and transformation in the journey of an ordinary character facing the challenges of modern life. »*

Fictionalized Biography:

*"I'd like a fictionalized biography of [a prominent historical figure], structured according to The Hero's Journey:*

1. *The Ordinary World (Childhood/Youth)*
2. *The Call to a Particular Destiny*
3. *First doubts/rejections in the face of this destiny*
4. *A Decisive Encounter/Mentor*
5. *First steps towards this vocation*
6. *The first tests and achievements*
7. *The approach to the work/major accomplishment*
8. *The Ultimate Challenge*
9. *The consecration/realization of one's work*
10. *The consequences of his legacy*
11. *A new philosophy of life*
12. *Legacy and lasting impact*

*Highlight the extraordinary journey of this character through the symbolic stages of the Hero's Journey. »*

Spy Thriller:

*"For this spy thriller, let's use the 12 stages of the Hero's Journey:*

1. *A secret agent in his routine*
2. *A special mission has been entrusted to it*
3. *At first, he was reluctant to accept*
4. *An informant or ally helps them prepare*
5. *He commits and takes action*
6. *First twists and turns of the mission*
7. *A discovery leads him to the heart of the conspiracy*
8. *Confronting the most formidable enemy*
9. *If he succeeds in his secret mission*
10. *Escape and chase to get out*
11. *A sacrifice or a change transforms it*
12. *The return, but with consequences to assume*

*Build a fast-paced spy plot where your hero will evolve through these perilous stages worthy of a great thriller. »*

Coming-of-age story:

*"For this tale of learning and initiation, let's follow the structure of The Hero's Journey:*

1. *Present the young protagonist in his daily life*
2. *An event challenges his view of the world*
3. *At first, he was reluctant to change*
4. *He meets a mentor/spiritual guide*
5. *He begins his initiatory journey*
6. *The First Revelations and Challenges*
7. *It reaches a point of no return*
8. *He has to face the ultimate test*
9. *He makes a discovery about himself*
10. *He's coming back, but nothing is the same anymore*

*11. A rebirth, a new beginning*

*12. His New Life with What He's Learned*

*Explore the journey of a young researcher confronted with the mysteries of existence through this initiatory journey in 12 steps. »*

These detailed prompts provide the AI with a clear framework for structuring an epic narrative that faithfully follows the 12 steps of the classic Hero's Journey pattern. Whether it's a fantasy, biographical, spy or coming-of-age story, this structure makes it possible to trace the complete arc of transformation of the heroic protagonist from the outset.

**The Fichtean Curve**

<u>Family Drama:</u>

*"I'd like you to develop the plot of this family drama in a way that respects the emotional structure of the Fichtean Curve:*

1. *Describe the initial tense situation within this family*
2. *Triggering Event Heightens Existing Tensions*
3. *Conflicts and unspoken things explode, tensions are at their highest*
4. *A liberating confrontation relieves the pressure*
5. *The epilogue exploring how the family can rebuild itself*

*Be sure to gradually build up the pressure to a dramatic and emotional peak, before you begin to recede and explore the consequences of this family storm. »*

<u>Dystopian Thriller:</u>

*"For this dystopian thriller, use the Fichtean Curve:*

1.  *Present the oppressive futuristic world as a backdrop*
2.  *An incident sows rebellion among the protagonists*
3.  *The hunt and confrontation escalate to a climax*
4.  *A great upheaval creates a power vacuum*
5.  *What new era is dawning after these violent changes?*

*Build a gradual plunge into extreme chaos, reaching a peak of revolutionary violence followed by a disturbing void that will need to be filled. »*


<u>Historical novel:</u>

*"Let's adopt the structure of Fichtean's Curve for this novel about the Renaissance:*

1.  *The Initial Situation: Court Life/Artists in the Shadows*
2.  *A creation/discovery challenges the established order*
3.  *Passionate research, heated debates, dangers*
4.  *The Apogee of the New Philosophy and Upheaval*
5.  *The lasting impact of this paradigm shift*

*Let the protagonists experience the slow emergence of the humanist spirit and the questioning, until the climax of confrontation with the old order, before exploring the major repercussions. »*

Coming-of-age story:

*"For this coming-of-age story, let's use the Fichtean Curve:*

1. *The protagonist's initial life, still full of illusions*
2. *The first doubts and questioning shake him*
3. *The search for answers intensifies, extreme tensions*
4. *A decisive revelation/experience transforms him*
5. *He returns to his world with a new philosophy*

*Start with a protagonist in denial, then take him through phases of increasingly marked doubts, until the final shock of a fundamental realization. »*

Coming-of-age novel:

*"Let us construct the structure of this novel according to the Fichtean Curve:*

1. *The protagonist's initially carefree adolescence*
2. *The first disappointments/disillusions reach him*
3. *Rebellion, conflict and confusion escalate*
4. *The final confrontation paves the way for maturity*
5. *He re-enters society with a new outlook*

*Follow the young character's evolution arc from carefree to the gradual torments and wanderings of adolescence, before a final conflict pushes him into adulthood. »*

**Y-structure**

<u>Multiple-choice narrative:</u>


*"For this interactive multiple-choice novel, let's adopt a Y-structure:*

1. *Introduce the initial setting and the protagonists*
2. *Up to the first fork where 2 options are available to the reader*
3. *Develop each branch in a balanced way*
4. *Converge the 2 branches to a new fork*
5. *Continue until you reach a common denouement to conclude*

*Offer regular choices that significantly change the flow of the plot, while ensuring that the different paths remain consistent before joining each other occasionally. »*


<u>Novel about free will:</u>

*"I'd like to explore the question of free will with a Y-structure:*

1. *The starting point: a protagonist faced with a dilemma*
2. *Describe the 2 options available to him, with their implications*
3. *Develop the path of each choice in depth*
4. *Converge the 2 paths to decisive consequences*
5. *The same final destiny, but different philosophical conclusions*

*Explore in depth the diametrically opposed implications of this fundamental choice, before a common conclusion that puts the importance of decisions into perspective. »*

<u>*Sociological Novel/Case Study:*</u>

*"Let's adopt a Y-structure for this sociological study of real cases:*

1. *Explain the problematic situation and societal issues*
2. *Present 2 representative cases with divergent trajectories*
3. *Follow in detail the evolution of each of these 2 cases*
4. *The protagonists' paths converge towards the same major crisis*
5. *Analyze the different possible social impacts depending on the outcome*

*Explore the contrasting and then converging trajectories of your study subjects, before putting into perspective the underlying sociological realities according to the outcomes. »*

<u>Dystopian Sci-Fi Novel:</u>

*"Let's use a Y-structure for this dystopia about an alternate future:*

1. *The political/technological situation that creates a historical bifurcation*
2. *The 2 radically different paths that are opening up for humanity*
3. *Describe each of the 2 parallel realities in an elaborate way*
4. *Bring the 2 branches together towards the same planetary crisis*
5. *What is the most plausible/desirable outcome?*

*Explore scenarios of opposite, yet believable, worlds before seeing how they lead to the same emergency requiring a common response. »*

Detective novel with multiple puzzles:

*"For this detective novel, let's use a Y-shaped tree structure:*

1. *The Initial Situation: A Murder Case to Solve*
2. *Two main suspects/motives are emerging*
3. *Follow the investigations around each suspect in detail*
4. *Both Investigations Converge on Difficult Evidence*
5. *How will the investigator ultimately solve the case?*

*Propose two solid criminal theories that the reader can follow in parallel, before a resolution where all the grey areas will be cleared up. »*

With this Y-structure allowing multiple narrative paths to be explored head-on, AI can develop branching plots where the choices of the reader or protagonists will have a real impact. As the different paths come together from time to time, this hybrid structure allows for narratives with multiple endings as well as more universal conclusions after contrasting paths.

**Circular structure**
Philosophical Novel/Existential Reflection:

*"I'd like a novel that develops a philosophical reflection on the meaning of existence with a circular structure:*

1. *The initial situation raises the protagonist's fundamental questions*
2. *His journey to find answers leads him down various paths*
3. *His journey brings him revelations, but also new doubts*
4. *A total questioning of one's certainties, a return to the starting point*
5. *The conclusion: a new perspective on these crucial questions*
6.

*Construct a narrative where the protagonist completes a complete loop in his existential quest, starting from the same question into which he will fall, but with a transformed gaze. »*

Historical Novel/Cycle of Civilizations:

*"Let's employ a cyclical structure for this historical novel about the evolution of civilizations:*

1. *The Founding of an Empire/Nascent Civilization*
2. *Follow its slow development, its dazzling golden age*
3. *Then its inevitable decline and its internal struggles*
4. *Its abrupt fall and return to barbarism/ruins*
5. *Lay the seeds of a new era/civilization to be born*

*Draw the complete arc of a civilization from its creation to its collapse, while establishing the cyclical conditions for a new society to rise from the ashes. »*


Initiatory Novel/Spiritual Quest:

*"For this spiritual and initiatory story, let's adopt a looping structure:*

1. *The protagonist aspires to transcendence, an initial situation*
2. *His journey to enlightenment leads him down various paths*
3. *Each new revelation leads to other challenges*
4. *His cycle of questioning brings him back to his starting point*
5. *He incorporates an absolute wisdom that goes beyond his primary questions*

*Through this circular journey, explore his evolution from a state of ignorance to a spiritual quest, and then transcend his original aspirations through what he will go through. »*

The circular narrative structure makes it possible to retrace a complete cycle, whether it is an initiatory quest, the destiny of a civilization, family or societal dynamics. Starting from the point of origin after a long journey, it offers the possibility of a deep final awareness of these loops to be reformed or transcended.

**Non-linear structure**

<u>Fragmented Narrative Novel/Narrative Puzzle:</u>

*"For this fragmented narrative novel, let's adopt a non-linear structure:*

1. *Establish the mysterious general framework of the plot to be reconstructed*
2. *Develop Narrative Sequences in a Messy Way*
3. *Each fragment brings new lighting/shadows*
4. *Some elements seem to contradict or intertwine*
5. *How do all the pieces fit together in the end?*

*Through an exploded narration, offer a real puzzle to the reader, who will have to reconstruct the chronology and the links between all the elements sown over the course of the non-linear sketches. »*

<u>Novel about memory/the journey of a lifetime:</u>

*"Let's employ a non-linear structure for this introspective novel about memory:*

1. *Pose the situation of the present: a protagonist reminisces about his life*
2. *Embark on a journey into his scattered and messy memories*
3. *Explore its defining phases, from childhood to its final days*
4. *Some parts are missing, contradict each other or take on a new meaning*
5. *What final truth emerges from this tormented memory?*

*Through temporal back-and-forth and fragmented narration, plunge into the depths of a psyche and a life whose pieces will gradually fall apart. »*

Initiatory travelogue/road trip:

"Let's adopt a fragmented structure for this coming-of-age travelogue:

1. The protagonist leaves his daily life for a journey
2. Suggest sketches of his road trip in no particular order
3. Each step brings a new lesson, a new step
4. Some experiences seem disconnected or paradoxical
5. How will this trip explode his vision of the world?

Through a kaleidoscopic narration, retrace the initiatory journey of your traveler through his labyrinthine encounters and discoveries. »


Psychological Thriller/Mental Drifts:

"For this psychological thriller, let's scramble with a messy narrative:

1. A protagonist seems to sink into a daze/madness
2. Describe his wobbly daily life in successive snippets
3. Alternate between anchored passages and unsealed anxiety-provoking perceptions
4. To what extent do his hallucinations become a reality?
5. What truth is hidden under the apparent mental drifts?

In the course of this unstructured narrative between the present and delirium, sow confusion between real facts and fabrications to better cover the tracks. »

Non-linear narration allows for multiple effects: arousing curiosity through a puzzle structure, exploring the meanders of the psyche through a quest for meaning through scattered memories, or modeling the perception of reality through a deconstructed chronology. These prompts guide the AI to imagine a bold narrative architecture that transcends convention.

# Chapter 10

# PROOFREADING AND EDITING WITH AI

# The importance of proofreading and editing

Writing a novel is a long and complex process that requires not only inspiration and creativity, but also rigorous proofreading and editing. This crucial step, often overlooked or minimized by first-time authors, is nevertheless essential to transform a promising draft into a successful and impactful work.

Proofreading and editing first identify and correct grammatical, spelling, and typographical errors that can harm the reader's understanding and tarnish the author's image. Even the most experienced writers are not immune to a slip of the tongue or careless mistake, and it is paramount to remove these imperfections before publication.

But beyond these purely technical aspects, proofreading and revision are also an opportunity to thoroughly rethink the narrative structure, the development of the characters, the coherence of the plot and the fluidity of the style. It is at this stage that the author can identify weaknesses in their narrative, inconsistencies, or lengths, and make any necessary changes to enhance the impact of their novel.

It is not uncommon, during this revision phase, to have to rework entire chapters, add or remove scenes, deepen certain characters or tighten the links between the different elements of the plot. This step can be arduous and frustrating, as it often involves questioning some of the work that has already been done. However, it is essential to give the work its full dimension and coherence.

Proofreading and editing also help fine-tune the writing style and find the most suitable narrative voice. This allows an author to spot awkward wording, superfluous repetitions, or overly long descriptions, and replace them with more elegant and impactful phrases. It's an opportunity to chisel out each sentence, find the right words and give the writing its personal touch.

Finally, it is crucial to submit your manuscript to external reviewers, whether they are relatives, other authors or publishing professionals. Their fresh and impartial perspective will allow them to detect the weaknesses that the author, too involved in his work, may have missed. Their comments and constructive criticism will be opportunities to improve the novel before it is published.

## Using AI to Identify Grammatical and Stylistic Errors

The use of artificial intelligence (AI) to identify grammatical and stylistic errors is a rapidly expanding field that offers many benefits. Modern AI models, trained on huge corpora of texts, are now able to detect grammar, spelling, syntax and even stylistic blunders with great accuracy.

This ability of AI to analyze and correct texts is a valuable asset for writers, students, professionals, and anyone concerned with producing quality written content. Indeed, writing a text that is free of errors can be a daunting task, even for the best authors. The human eye tends to miss certain mistakes, especially after several proofreadings of the same document.

That's where AI comes in. Thanks to its powerful machine learning algorithms, it is able to analyze every sentence, every word, and detect the slightest imperfections with formidable precision. AI tools such as online grammar checkers or word processing extensions can spot the most subtle errors, ranging from chord mistakes to punctuation issues to awkward wording.

Beyond simple correction, some AI models can even suggest stylistic improvements. For example, they identify sentences that are too long or complex, unnecessary repetitions, approximate phrases, and propose clearer and more elegant reformulations. This feature is especially useful for authors who want to refine their style and make their writing flow and enjoyable to read.

AI doesn't just fix existing mistakes, it can also prevent potential mistakes. Some AI-assisted writing tools flag grammatical or stylistic issues in real-time as the user writes their text. This avoids accumulating errors and facilitates subsequent revision.

Nevertheless, despite its incredible performance, AI is not infallible and cannot fully replace human judgment. They can sometimes make mistakes or propose inappropriate corrections, especially in complex or idiomatic contexts. That's why it's recommended to use AI as a writing tool, maintaining critical thinking and manually validating the suggestions offered.

Overall, using AI to identify grammatical and stylistic errors is a major step forward in improving the quality of writing. By offering accurate and exhaustive automated proofreading, it allows everyone to produce neat and professional texts, regardless of their level of language proficiency or writing skills. In the all-digital age, this technology is an undeniable asset for standing out for the quality of one's writing.

# Narrative optimization and plot coherence with AI

Thanks to their data analysis and processing capabilities, AI systems are becoming valuable allies for authors who want to create rich, captivating stories that are free of inconsistencies.

One of the first advantages of AI for writing is its ability to detect inconsistencies and contradictions within a story. By analyzing the entire text, these systems can spot elements that don't add up, whether it's in terms of chronology, character characteristics, or plot details. They then point out these inconsistencies to the author, allowing him to correct them and thus strengthen the overall coherence of his work.

But AI doesn't just point out problems, it can also suggest solutions to fix them. Thanks to its extensive databases and learning algorithms, it is able to propose alternative narrative tracks, character adjustments, or plot changes that preserve the logic and fluidity of the narrative. The author retains creative control, of course, but the AI gives him an array of relevant options to optimize his story.

Another valuable contribution of AI is character development. By analyzing their character traits, motivations, and actions as the story unfolds, AI systems can detect behavioral inconsistencies and suggest adjustments to make characters more believable and memorable. They can also identify stereotypes or clichés to avoid, helping authors create rich, nuanced characters.

AI can also play a crucial role in the overall narrative structure. By looking at the sequence of events, highlights, and twists and turns, she can gauge the balance and pacing of the plot. If some parts lack dynamism or if others are too dense, the AI will suggest ways to optimize, such as adding twists and turns or rearranging certain sequences, to ensure a captivating narrative from start to finish.

Finally, AI can also help enrich the fictional universe by providing detailed and accurate information about specific historical, geographical, or scientific contexts. Drawing on its extensive knowledge bases, it will allow authors to ground their stories in believable and detail-rich environments, bringing an extra dimension of realism and immersion to the reader.

## Using a Scan Prompt

By using AI as a personal assistant, you would benefit from a powerful tool to analyze, optimize, and polish your novel at every stage of the writing process. Of course, you'd retain the final creative control, but the AI would offer you sound advice and relevant suggestions to elevate the quality of your artwork to the next level.

To begin analyzing your novel with AI, you must first upload your manuscript. To do this, locate the paperclip icon in the interface and click on it. A window will then open allowing you to select your novel file in Microsoft Word (.doc) or PDF format from your computer. Once you have chosen the file, validate the download.

When the manuscript is successfully uploaded, an input field will appear to enter your analysis prompt. It is in this area that you will be able to copy and paste or directly type the detailed prompt describing the desired analyses and optimizations for your novel, as we wrote it previously.

**Quick**

To get the most out of AI analytics and optimization capabilities for your novel, it's best to provide it with a clear and detailed prompt. Here's how you might phrase this prompt:

*"Hello, I'd like you to take an in-depth look at my novel [Novel Title] in order to optimize its narrative structure, plot coherence, and character development.*

*Here's what I expect from your analysis:*

*Performs an overall assessment of narrative structure: pacing, balance of events, highlights, twists and turns, etc. Let me know which parts need to be reworked and suggest ways to improve the flow of the story.*

*Analyzes the consistency of the main characters [Character Names]: motivations, character traits, behaviors, evolution, etc. Points out inconsistencies and suggests adjustments to make them more believable and memorable.*

*Spot any inconsistencies, contradictions, or missing details in the plot, timeline, descriptions, etc. And make suggestions to me to correct these problems.*

*Identifies redundant passages, lengths, or superfluous scenes to be cut for a smoother narrative.*

*Suggests alternative narrative paths, added twists and turns, or rearranged sequences to make the story more engaging.*

*Finally, proofread carefully to correct grammatical, spelling, and typographical errors.*

*I enclose the complete manuscript of my novel. Feel free to ask me questions if you need clarification. I'm open to all your suggestions for optimization, but I'll keep the final say on the changes to be made. »*

By providing these clear instructions with the specific elements of your novel, you'll help the AI perform an in-depth and personalized analysis. Don't forget to attach the full manuscript. The AI will be able to offer you expert advice on how to refine your work, while leaving you in control for the final creative decisions. Feel free to adjust the prompt to your specific needs.

Chapter 11

# THE LAYOUT

## Preparation

Although AI can generate the texts, you will have to take care of the layout and preparation of the manuscript for printing yourself. I will provide you with advice using the word processing software Word, which is widely used for this type of task, as an example. Microsoft Word is a paid software that is part of the Microsoft Office suite, available as a subscription or one-time purchase. However, Microsoft also offers a free online version called "Word Online" (**https://www.microsoft.com/microsoft-365/word**), which can be accessed through your web browser with a Microsoft account (Hotmail, Outlook, etc.). This online version offers the basic functionality needed to create and edit text documents. So, even if you don't own the full paid version, you'll be able to do the final layout of your AI-generated novel through *"Word Online."*

Depending on the length of your novel, we recommend using one of the preformatted layout templates available on our exclusive platform for book buyers. These free templates, specially designed for self-publishing, already incorporate the right margins, page numbering as well as essential preliminary pages like the table of contents. They will make it easy for you to prepare your manuscript for professional publication, whether on Amazon KDP or other online sales platforms. By acquiring our must-have guide, you'll gain access to this library of must-have resources to successfully complete your AI-assisted self-publishing project.

## Essential Layout Tips

When you decide to write a self-published book, the layout is a crucial element in ensuring an enjoyable reading experience. Here are some tips to help you create a professional and engaging book:

### Stick to the Headmatter

Introductory pages, also known as endpapers, are the very first pages of your book and play a vital role in the overall impression it conveys. Usually composed of the fake title page, the title page, and the legal notice, these introductory pages are an opportunity to lay the foundation of your story and formalize your status as a published author.

**False title page:** Formerly known as the "cover page," this page typically includes the title of the work in modestly sized letters. Usually located on page 5 (or page 7 if there is a table of contents), it plays a crucial role in the structure of your work.

**Title page:** The title page, which has temporarily replaced the term "cover page", highlights the name of the author, the title of the work and, if applicable, its subtitle.

Legal notices, including copyright, manufacturing information (e.g. year of publication, rights holder, publisher, printer and ISBN), are relegated to the imprint pages.

It is important to note that all of these front matter pages are an integral part of the pagination, although the page number should not appear on them. This practice standardizes the entire book and makes it easier for the reader to navigate.

Harmonize the presentation of your text by justifying it (alignment of the two margins) and ensuring that each new chapter always starts on an odd page. This approach ensures a neat aesthetic and a fluid reading, thus improving the experience of your readership.

Admittedly, the standards for the presentation and composition of a literary work are broader and more nuanced. However, by applying these initial tips, you will be able to craft an engaging and beautifully crafted novel that will satisfy both your requirements and those of your readership.

# Author-AI Symbiosis: Direction and Adaptation

Even if you're using AI to write, it's essential to stay in control of your work. Feel free to direct, guide, or instruct the AI throughout the process. You can provide them with ideas, suggestions, direction, or even write a paragraph yourself and then ask them to build on that paragraph or idea.

Here are some prompt suggestions to guide AI towards more personalized writing:

*"Describe the main character's deepest thoughts and emotions when faced with a crucial moral dilemma."*

*"Imagine a poignant scene where the main character reminisces about a key moment in his childhood that shaped his personality."*

*"Write a dialogue between two main characters that reveals their secret motivations and internal conflicts."*

*"Creates an immersive description of an important place in the story, using all the senses to capture the atmosphere and emotion."*


*"Develops an inner monologue from the main character as he struggles with his doubts and fears before a crucial event."*


*"Imagine a series of flashbacks that shed light on a supporting character's complex past and influence their present behavior."*


*"Write a thrilling action scene where the main character's unique skills are put to the test in a face-to-face encounter with adversity."*

Chapter 12

# AI and the Future of Publishing

# Democratization of writing

The artificial intelligence revolution is no longer limited to technological or scientific fields. It now goes to the very heart of one of the noblest and most ancestral arts: writing. Far from the fears of some purists, this disruption promoted by AI is not intended to replace writers, but rather to democratize access to literary creation.

For centuries, the world of publishing has been governed by strict codes, shaped by a small elite of publishing houses. This closed industry too often confined new talent to the shadow of established authors. The advent of self-publishing was a first breach, but technical and financial challenges remained a hindrance for many creators.

This is where artificial intelligence comes in as a powerful lever for democratization. By offering affordable and intuitive writing assistance tools, it drastically lowers the barrier to entry. Now, anywhere in the world, anyone with a computer or smartphone can embark on the adventure of creative writing, regardless of their level of education or background.

AI-suggested writing prompts can infuse a real narrative dynamic into a project under construction. Plot and character generators provide inspiration for aspiring authors. Combined with a natural conversational interface, AI becomes a valuable creative partner, a benevolent guide to give shape to the craziest stories.

But AI is not limited to the role of facilitator. It also paves the way for new emerging writing styles, innovative and hybrid literary formulas. The boundaries between written narratives and narratives generated by artificial intelligence are becoming more and more porous, to the point of sometimes becoming blurred. A true creative renaissance is on the horizon.

This democratization is not limited to amateur writers. It also offers a new lease of life for published authors, who can renew their approach and explore new genres, galvanized by AI's suggestions. A real mix of styles and influences is underway.

Publishing is no longer reserved for the privileged of yesterday. With its revolutionary accessibility, artificial intelligence is propelling it into an era of unprecedented creative diversity. A whole section of the population can now legitimately claim the status of writer and hope to reach the public with original works. A wave of once-stifled talent is about to unleash. AI has definitively opened the floodgates of literary democratization.

# When AI becomes the pen of authors

We've always seen writing as an ultra-personal and creative thing, where the author chooses each word carefully in a moment of artistic solitude. But times are changing! A real revolution is coming to the literary world and artificial intelligence is no longer just an assistant, it is starting to co-write with authors.

The first signs of this upheaval are already there. With text generators, creators can give the outline of a story – the setting, main characters, etc. And the AI then takes care of enriching this canvas with breathtaking descriptions, hard-hitting dialogues and crazy twists! A real teamwork between human and machine.

This marriage gives rise to completely hybrid narratives where writing styles mix and reinvent themselves. The AI's overflowing imagination boosts the writer's pen with crazy plots and totally singular atmospheres. A wind of creativity and originality is blowing through literature!

And this creative upheaval is not limited to the realm of fictional novels. Writing augmented by artificial intelligence is also making its way into other literary territories such as poetry or essays. Machines show a disconcerting agility in handling subtle language games, deploying striking metaphors and developing philosophical reflections of unsuspected depth, sometimes on themes that are a priori unexpected.

Their creativity seems to know no established boundaries, challenging many preconceived ideas about the truly limited capacities of the artificial mind. This poetic and conceptual exploration by artificial intelligence pushes the limits of written expression in directions that have not yet been suspected.

This human-machine duo isn't just changing writing techniques. It turns the creative act itself upside down! Writing becomes a thing in constant evolution, a real permanent dialogue between the two creators. The story is built and transformed over the course of the exchanges.

In this new situation, the lines are blurred. Who is really the final author? Does the inspiration come from the AI that forms the text or from the human who laid the foundations? It raises big philosophical and legal questions about originality and literary authorship.

But one thing is for sure, AI-augmented writing doesn't herald the end of artistic creation. On the contrary, it's the opening up to crazy new creative territories, at the crossroads of art and techno. Authors will have to fully embark on this wave of change in their ancestral profession. A total revolution in sight, the atmospheres!

# The Revival of AI Publishing

Traditional book publishing is often seen as an obstacle course for an author. Whether it's persuading a publisher of the value of their manuscript or complying with various editorial requirements, the path can be complex and discouraging. However, changing practices in the sector now offer promising alternatives.

Currently, we are witnessing a significant transformation in the field of book distribution, thanks to the emergence of print-on-demand, an innovation amplified by artificial intelligence. This revolution is reshaping the very foundations of the publishing industry.

The foundation of this innovation is based on a relatively straightforward idea. State-of-the-art printers, connected to digital platforms, now allow individual books to be printed on demand, eliminating the need for mass production and large inventories. Whether the book is aimed at a niche audience or is of a more confidential nature, it is now available for sale without any minimum quantity constraints.

The introduction of artificial intelligence into this process opens up even wider horizons. Thanks to its advanced algorithms, AI is able to take over a large part of editorial tasks that previously required significant human intervention. From layout to spell checking, to cover design, AI makes the publishing journey much easier, allowing authors to fully focus on the creative side of their work.

As a result, any writer, even with little experience in layout, can easily dispense with publishers and choose self-publishing for their novel, comic book, or poetry collection. The best part is that it can pass on this increase in productivity to the selling price for its readers!

The direct consequence is a considerable literary diversity that will flood the shelves. No more standardized commercial bestsellers to please as many people as possible. Instead, we are witnessing a delightful flowering of offbeat, avant-garde works imbued with unbridled creativity.

Naturally, like any major change, this leads to some reluctance on the part of the publishing giants. They take a dim view of this breeze of freedom blowing over their traditionally very closed business. But there's no turning back in the face of such a wave!

Authors finally have the means to shape their literary destiny. Say goodbye to serial rejections and creative and painful compromises. Welcome to a new world where originality and creative audacity are valued! A veritable cultural revolution is brewing in the shadows, punctuated by the joyful hum of on-demand printers. An exciting publishing era is on the horizon!

# Authors 2.0: Independence through AI

The emancipation of writers through technology reaches a new level with artificial intelligence. Until now, the self-publishing movement already represented significant progress, allowing authors to free themselves from the tutelage of traditional publishing houses. However, this path remained fraught with technical and practical constraints.

The advent of AI-augmented writing tools is removing these last hurdles. Authors will soon have a complete ecosystem that allows them to carry out the entire creative process autonomously, from idea generation to shelving.

Assisted by these high-performance artificial intelligences, the construction of sophisticated plots, the writing of natural dialogues and the development of nuanced characters will no longer hold any secrets. AI will offer inexhaustible creative resources to nurture and stimulate writers' inspiration.

But his role will not be limited to this writing aid. It will also take on the toughest tasks of formatting, editing, and promoting with increased productivity. From book covers to hyper-targeted marketing campaigns, including meticulous layout, everything will be orchestrated with dexterity.

A truly integrated and fully automated editorial platform will thus take shape around the writers, offering them total creative and commercial independence. This major break with the classic model of publishing will allow them to be fully masters of their literary destiny.

While an adaptation phase was undeniably necessary, the gain in freedom and creative serenity would be substantial for the authors. No more painful artistic compromises, unfair financial compensations or stifling commercial logics to endure. Just the expression of their pure art, nourished by the precious assistance of artificial intelligence.

A paradigm shifts of major significance for the literary sphere, which would mark the advent of a new creative Renaissance. An unprecedented opportunity for writers to break through and find their audience in the digital age, while remaining fully faithful to their artistic line.

Chapter 13

# Extra income thanks to AI

# Extra income

Writing books is often seen as a passion rather than a source of income. Still, in today's digital age, it can prove to be a worthwhile investment, especially with the rise of online sales platforms such as Amazon. The equation seems simple: the more you write, the more you sell, and the more the monthly royalties increase. This dynamic creates an unprecedented opportunity for authors to generate substantial passive income through their works.

The advent of artificial intelligence (AI) tools in the field of writing is opening up new avenues for authors, allowing them to maximize their creative and commercial potential. These ever-evolving technologies offer valuable assistance in the writing process, from ideation to writing, and even in the go-to-market phase. They help overcome some of the traditional challenges associated with writing books, such as writer's block or intensive research, making the process smoother and less time-consuming.

The key to profitability lies in the ability to produce content on a regular basis. Each book published represents a potential new source of income. In Amazon's competitive marketplace, visibility is crucial. Having multiple titles under your belt not only increases an author's visibility, but also improves their attractiveness to potential readers.

Amazon's recommendation algorithms favor authors with multiple works, increasing the chances of cross-selling between different titles.

In addition, the multiplication of titles makes it possible to build a loyal base of readers. Each new book is an opportunity to strengthen ties with its audience, who, seduced by a work, are more inclined to discover others. This virtuous cycle can significantly increase monthly royalties, turning writing an expensive hobby into a lucrative business.

Writing books, especially with the help of AI, thus becomes a viable strategy for generating passive income. Although not all authors can make a living exclusively from their writing, many manage to build up a significant additional monthly income. This additional source of income can be a significant part of the monthly budget, providing financial freedom and allowing authors to devote more time to their passion.

It's important to note that success doesn't come overnight. It requires determination, perseverance, and a consistent publishing strategy. Using AI tools wisely to optimize content and productivity can speed up the process, but the key is quality and engagement with your audience.

Writing books, supported by AI tools, offers an unprecedented opportunity for aspiring and established authors to capitalize on the growing demand for content on platforms like Amazon. By embracing this new era of digital publishing, authors can turn their passion into a source of passive income, or even a full-fledged career. The key to success lies in the ability to consistently produce quality content, thus exploiting the full potential of each published work.

# Key Strategies for Selling AI Books on Amazon

Selling books created with the help of artificial intelligence (AI) on Amazon requires a strategic approach to stand out in a crowded market. Here are five essential strategies to maximize your chances of success:

## 1. Amazon Search Engine Optimization (SEO)

Amazon is first and foremost a search engine for book buyers. Optimization for Amazon is crucial. Use relevant keywords in your book's title, description, and metadata to ensure it appears in potential readers' search results. Conduct research to identify the most searched keywords in your genre and incorporate them in a natural way.

Artificial intelligence (AI) can play a crucial role in optimizing your book's visibility on Amazon, especially by helping you identify relevant keywords that appeal to your target audience. AI-based tools analyze vast data sets to understand current search trends, readers' interests, and the language used by similar books that perform well. This analysis helps identify strategic keywords that your audience is likely to use when searching. By incorporating these keywords into your book's title, subtitle, and description, you increase the chances that Amazon will present it to potentially interested readers. AI can also identify gaps or opportunities in specific niches, helping you uniquely position your book in the market.

For the writing of an impactful description, AI can assist by generating draft text that captures the essence of your book while incorporating copywriting best practices. These technologies can suggest effective description structures, intriguing catchphrases, and compelling calls to action, while ensuring that content remains optimized for Amazon's search engines. By using AI to fine-tune tone and style, you can create a description that not only resonates with your audience, but also highlights the unique aspects of your book. This helps to increase interest from potential readers, improve conversions, and ultimately boost your book's sales on Amazon.

## 2. Creating Attractive and Professional Covers

The cover is the first thing that catches buyers' attention. Invest in a professional cover design that communicates the genre and tone of your book in a visual way. A well-designed cover not only increases the visibility of your book but also improves the perception of its quality by potential buyers. It is also possible to ask the artificial intelligence to create the cover of your novel. Since the AI created the novel with you, it has control over its content, so it will be easier for it to create a cover art that represents your work well.

Here's an example of a prompt for your cover design:

"Create an image for my novel. The image must have a resolution of 6 x 9 inches (or whatever size you choose for your novel). It has to reflect the essence of my novel. I want a clean, artistic style."

Feel free to give them more instructions and details.

In addition, I asked for the creation of an "image" rather than a novel cover. When a request for a cover is made, it often results in a book-like illustration like this picture.

## 3. Leveraging Amazon's Marketing Tools

Amazon offers a range of marketing tools for authors, including paid ads (Amazon Ads), free or discounted book promotions, and the Kindle Unlimited program. These tools can increase your book's visibility to a wider audience. Paid ads, in particular, can be an effective way to target specific readers interested in your genre.

Artificial intelligence (AI) can transform your approach to paid ads on Amazon (Amazon Ads) by making your campaigns more effective and targeted. With AI, you can analyze massive amounts of data on consumer behavior, search trends, and previous ad performance to optimize your ad campaigns. AI algorithms can predict which keywords will drive the most traffic to your book, when ads should run to reach the maximum number of users, and what budget to allocate to maximize ROI. Additionally, AI can automate the A/B testing process, allowing different versions of an ad to be compared to determine which one performs best. This ability to adapt and learn in real-time can significantly increase the effectiveness of your Amazon listings, attracting more potential readers to your book.

When it comes to Amazon's marketing tools, AI can help personalize user experiences and improve the visibility of your promotions. For example, it can analyze customers' buying habits and reading preferences to recommend your book to specific market segments that may be interested. AI can also optimize email marketing campaigns by segmenting email lists and personalizing email content to increase open and conversion rates. In addition, using AI chatbots to engage customers on social media platforms or on your website can provide instant support, answer questions about your book, and promote your special offers interactively. By incorporating AI into your Amazon marketing strategy, you can not only reach a wider audience, but also create more personalized and effective ad campaigns.

## 4. Creating a Book Series

Creating a book series can significantly increase your sales on Amazon, mainly because the series generate ongoing engagement from readers. When a reader delves into the first book in a series and gets attached to the characters, universe, or plot, they are much more likely to want to continue reading the subsequent volumes to see how the story develops. This commitment creates anticipation for new releases, which can lead to cumulative sales with each new addition to the series. In addition, series offer the opportunity to create a more complex and rewarding narrative arc, which may not be possible in the context of a single book. This can make your series more appealing to readers looking for an immersive and extended reading experience, increasing the chances of positive recommendations and reviews, which are crucial for visibility on Amazon.

Also, from a marketing perspective, book series offer strategic advantages on Amazon. For example, readers who buy the first book are high-value leads for subsequent volumes, allowing for more effective targeted marketing campaigns, such as follow-up emails or cross-promotions between books in the series. Amazon itself favors series through its recommendation algorithms, because the sale of complete series increases the average basket of purchases. The series also allow you to organize promotions such as making the first volume free to attract new readers, or creating bundles at a reduced price. These techniques can not only increase the visibility of your series, but also create a ripple effect, where the popularity of one book fuels interest in the other volumes, creating a self-sustaining sales dynamic on the Amazon platform.

## 5. Engagement and Community Building

Engagement and community building are fundamental to the success of a self-published book. Social media platforms, such as TikTok and Facebook, offer unique opportunities to reach and interact with a targeted audience. TikTok, with its dynamic nature and virality-promoting algorithm, allows authors to create creative and engaging content around their book. Short videos featuring readings, anecdotes about the writing process, or even challenges related to the theme of the book can capture users' attention and pique their interest. The visual and interactive aspect of TikTok encourages sharing, increasing the book's visibility to a wider audience.

Facebook, on the other hand, offers a platform to build a strong community around the book. Facebook groups allow authors to gather interested readers, share updates, excerpts, or host Q&A sessions. This creates a sense of belonging and personal engagement among readers, which is crucial for encouraging word-of-mouth. In addition, Facebook Ads offers precise targeting tools, allowing self-publishing authors to promote their book to specific segments of the population that are likely to be interested. By using these platforms strategically, focusing on creating authentic and engaging content, authors can significantly increase their visibility and attract a loyal audience, which is essential for selling your novel.

**Bonus: Keep innovating with AI**

AI is rapidly evolving. Stay on top of the latest technological advancements that could improve the quality of your writing or offer new ways to create and promote your books. The innovative use of AI can not only improve the efficiency of your writing process but also serve as a single selling point for your marketing.

By incorporating these strategies into your publishing and marketing plan, you can significantly increase your chances of success in selling AI-created books on Amazon. The key is to stay adaptable, continually learn from your publishing experiences, and adjust your strategies accordingly to maximize your reach and revenue.

I also encourage you to visit Ai BEYOND THE PEN's website, where I regularly share technological discoveries and tips on using artificial intelligence to write and promote your novel.

# Chapter 14

# The BEYOND THE PEN

# The website

The web portal "AI BEYOND THE PEN[5]" is an essential supplement to this manual for the development of a novel with the support of artificial intelligence. This website, which is regularly updated, offers a wealth of ideas and tools designed to make it easier to write your book using AI.

## Authoring Interface

To offer you the best possible support, I have designed a tailor-made artificial intelligence that will guide you in the creation of your book, accompanying you step by step. This AI encapsulates all of the principles discussed in this guide, providing you with comprehensive assistance in completing your project. The site offers a range of free resources, including prompt suggestions, original ideas, ratings on the different artificial intelligences available on the market and their progress. You'll also learn about a specific tool for designing the cover of your novel, including the back cover, in addition to various other tools discussed in this manual *(such as ready-to-use layout templates for Amazon)*. To top it all off, the site provides you with a handy guide to publishing your novel on Amazon.

---

[5] https://aidigitalpen.com

## Prompts

A wide range of pre-designed prompts are available to choose from, opening up a limitless field of possibilities to enrich your characters, design fascinating settings, and weave captivating storylines. Whether you're looking for inspiration to start a new novel or looking for strategies to improve the visibility of your books on platforms like Amazon, artificial intelligence can prove to be a valuable companion in the adventure of writing and marketing your works.

## Trainings

The world of artificial intelligence is constantly evolving and evolving. To support you in this dynamic, we have a section dedicated to training, where you can continue to explore new techniques for writing novels and discover the most effective strategies to sell your books on Amazon thanks to AI. You'll also have access to frequently updated articles that will provide you with up-to-date information about the world of artificial intelligence, whether specifically applied to writing or AI more generally. In addition, you will be able to connect to our various social media presences, offering you the opportunity to continue your training and participate in live writing sessions, exclusively reserved for our members and readers who have acquired this book.

## The Cover Page

An essential element not covered in this book, but accessible on our site, is the design of your cover. Whether you need a flyleaf or a back cover, artificial intelligence is capable of creating the design of your book. She can also assist you in developing an enticing description for your novel, aimed at captivating the attention of potential readers, and help you write a short biography of the author to include in the back of your book.

**The website**

To access these resources, simply register on "The BEYOND THE PEN" (**https://aidigitalpen.com**). By purchasing this book, you get free privileged access to our VIP section. To take advantage of this, please insert the promotional code " **authorai** " in the "promo code" box when registering.


In addition to exclusive content, you'll also get a 50% discount on all subscriptions available on our site.

9 798324 118020